THE BEAUTY OF
Horses

Triune Books

THE BEAUTY OF
Horses

by Peter Roberts

ISBN 0 85674 002 0
Published by
Triune Books, London, England
© Trewin Copplestone Publishing Ltd 1972
Colour and monochrome origination by City
Engraving Co (Hull) Ltd, England
Printed in Great Britain by Sir Joseph Causton
& Sons Ltd, London and Eastleigh
Second impression, 1973

Acknowledgments

Photographs were supplied by the following:

Daily Mirror: 6, 8; Calgary Stampede (Jack de Lorme): 9, 11, 13, 14; Austrian
National Tourist Office: 16*l*, 16*r*, 17, 18*l*, 20*r*; 21, 23*l*, 23*r*, 68; A.Q.H.A.: 26*t*, 26*b*,
27 (all), 30; National Film Board of Canada: 10, 93; Peter Sweetman: 35*t*; Rand
Sport & Press: 37*tl*; Judith Campbell: 15; Godfrey Argent: 39, 40, 41, 42, 43,
44 (all), 103*br*; Punch: 45*l*; Derek Davies: 47*r*; John Nestle: 47*l*, 125*r*, 135; Estall:
51*b*, 49; Monty: 6*c*, 107*bl*; Appaloosa H.C.: 63, 65, 66; Bill Crosby: 75*b*,; Julian
Graham: 77; Keystone: 83*lr*; Institut Belge d'Information: 87*b*; Bryan Conway: 86*t*;
Sport and General: 87*rl*, 102, 103*bl*, 103*tr*, 105*b*; French Tourist Office: 89*tl*;
Forestry Commission: 91*l*; Commissioner of Police: 92*r*; Spanish National Tourist
Office: 95*l*, 97*tl*; Elisabeth Weiland: 95*br*, 97*bl*, 97*tr*; Scottish Tourist Board: 86, 99*l*;
Swiss National Tourist Office: 99*t*; Press Association: 103*tl*; Leslie Lane: 107*t*, 108,
126*l*, 126*r*; Cape Argus: 131*t*; Riding: 69, 70, 138, 139, 140, 142, 143; Spectrum: 53;
Peter Roberts: 7, 18*r*, 19*l*, 19*r*, 20*l*, 24*t*, 24*b*, 32*tl*, 32*tr*, 33*b*, 33*l*, 33*tr*, 33*br*, 34*b*, 35*bl*,
35*br*, 36*t*, 36*b*, 37*tr*, 37*bl*, 37*br*, 48, 51*t*, 52, 54, 55, 56, 57*t*, 57*b*, 58(all), 59*t*, 59*b*,
60(all), 61*t*, 61*b*, 64, 73, 82, 84*l*, 84*r*, 86*br*, 87*l*, 88, 89*tr*, 89*b*, 96, 97*br*, 98(all), 100*bl*,
100*br*, 106, 107*br*, 109*t*, 111*l*, 111*r*, 112*t*, 114, 115*t*, 115*c*, 116, 117*t*, 117*r*, 118*bl*, 118*br*,
120, 121*t*, 123, 125*t*, 127*t*, 127*b*, 138*t*, 128*b*, 129*t*, 129*b*, 130*t*, 130*b*, 131*l*, 131*r*,
132(all), 133(all), 134, 135, 137, 141, 144.

Contents

The Beauty of Horses
Edited by Peter Roberts

Where in this wide world can man find nobility without pride, friendship without envy, or beauty without vanity? Here: where grace is laced with muscle, and strength by gentleness confined.

He serves without servility; he has fought without emnity. There is nothing so powerful, nothing less violent; there is nothing so quick, nothing more patient.

England's past has been born on his back. All our history is his industry. We are his heirs; he our inheritance.

      The Horse.

Ronald Duncan

The Wild Horses from Prehistory

The meadows stretch as far as the eye can see, dotted here and there with trees and small Spring flowers. The sun blazes down on the scene, and no noise disturbs the quiet rustle of hoof on grass.

At first glance there is nothing to commend the small horses standing peacefully in the field, or the nearby foals, who are behaving like foals anywhere in the world. But the horses *are* different. They are specimens from pre-history, hardly changed in form through a thousand generations . . .

The primitive paintings on the walls of a cave-dweller's home 10,000 years ago often depicted hunting scenes. In many of them were animals resembling the horse. They had short thick necks, bristly manes and high-set eyes, but were unmistakably equine. Not much to look at, certainly without the features to qualify for a beautiful-horse contest of modern times.

Yet they were the ancestors of a noble breed. Since their day, before history began, horses have changed over the years with infusions of blood and changing climates, evolving into many different breeds from the fleet Arabian to the gentle Percheron.

Or we should say, *most* horses have changed. One did not—the Mongolian Wild Horse. This one still roams the plains of outer Mongolia, where China meets Russia. He alone has remained unchanged, the world's last true wild horse.

Curiously, he was not 'discovered' until 1881 when Colonel Nicolai Przewalski (call it Pruz-al-ski) saw a herd of animals wandering in the distance when he was in a desert region of western Mongolia.

Realising that they were neither domestic horses escaped and turned wild, nor wild donkeys, he decided to investigate. But it was some time before a small herd could be captured and brought back from the Gobi desert to be examined and observed by zoologists.

Przewalski Horses graze in an English meadow.

A number of zoological gardens have small collections of these wild horses (now called Przewalski's Horses) and most are thriving. A small 'open' zoo in Russia has a herd, and at the Prague Zoo they keep a 'Wild Horse' record book to log the numbers of these rare horses all over the world. A few years back there were just 57 Przewalski's Horses and 69 mares—a slender thread on which to continue the line.

At Whipsnade Zoo in England—a great open park-zoo—a number are thriving and producing offspring. They seem to enjoy the rich pasture of the Bedfordshire countryside, just north of London, and, after a long history of desert living, who would blame them?

But they still look as though they have just stepped out of a cave-wall painting . . . the small, gentle eyes, high in the head, the brush-like mane, shaggy or bristly, depending on the season, and the large, rather ungainly head. Their coats are a reddish brown in summer with a marked dorsal stripe; in winter they become darker and the stripe less defined.

Even after years of living in the quiet parkland, the Przewalski Horse is *still* a real wild horse. Gentle in appearance, he may let a visitor near for a few moments—then this sole surviving ancestor of the domestic horse will wheel round and gallop off into the distance, well out of the range of humans . . .

Broncs, Chuckwagons, Wild Horses, Steer Wrestling . . .

Rodeo!

Cowboys line the fence on a hot, dusty day. The broncs in the chutes are quiet but tense. Sweat streaks their rough hides. The crowd are expectant, tense, waiting for the rodeo to begin. The first competitor, astride his bronc in the chute, leans down to test the flank strap cautiously. Every muscle in that horse is quivering. The judges are statues in the arena.

First bronc out, the cowboy jarred and spurring. Ten seconds to stay on . . . the horse is twisting, jack-knifing, its big body hurtling through the air—nostrils wide as it grunts, swerves, feints . . . ten seconds. The whistle blows and it's a question of getting the cowboy off. The judge on the steady buckskin pounds beside the frantic bronc. Almost casually he leans over and loosens the flank on the other horse; the cowboy grasps him round the waist and hauls himself over on to the buckskin's haunches; for a moment he is spread-eagled between the two horses, his legs flailing; then he scrambles down, falls to his knees, staggers for a moment and then jerks himself upright, grinning dustily. He made it! Cheers and laughter from his friends and rivals on the fence. The bronc has slowed to a jagged trot, his head high as he looks for the exit. It was a good ride.

Rodeo has five major events: saddle bronc riding **(above),** bareback riding, bull riding, steer wrestling and calf roping.

Why does a man become a cowboy? It is a tough life; it means broken bones, danger, sometimes long spells in hospital. Entry fees are between fifty and one hundred dollars for each competition and only a first-rate cowboy can hope to earn the peak rewards of around thirty-five thousand dollars a year. For most, the average is little more than three thousand. The successful cowboy may own an aeroplane, in which case his life becomes a frenetic merry-go-round on the rodeo circuit; he competes in as many as ninety rodeos a year and sometimes travels thousands of miles in a single day to attend two rodeos at opposite ends of the country. Some cowboys club together to buy an aeroplane but the majority travel overland as best they can. For them all, the expenses incurred are enormous—hotel bills, equipment, often hospital fees and time off for injuries.

What then is the attraction of rodeo? Maybe a cowboy becomes a cowboy because his father was one before him, or perhaps because he was bitten by the rodeo bug when he was a kid and found he could sit on some mean little bucking pony or a half-grown steer. Above all, rodeo offers independence; a man struts with his head high and relies only on his own skill. It is a true sport; most of the cowboys know each other well and are good friends in spite of the fierce competition. They are proud and honourable and would never think of 'doing the dirty' on each other. Rodeo cannot be a lifetime career; a cowboy will have only about six years when he is at his peak. Like an athlete he is in his prime from the age of about twenty-two to twenty-eight. A very few will remain fit enough to compete until they are thirty-five to forty, until the day the bull spins too quickly, or the bronc bucks too hard, and they are down with the hardest crash they ever took.

Prince of Horses

The wild and woolly bronc is one of the most pampered animals alive. More care is taken of him than of an expensive thoroughbred racehorse, and he will probably work for less than five minutes a year. Many broncs are owned by contractors; there are about ten major contractors that supply stock at all the big rodeos. As a rule the best bucking horses are spoilt saddle horses that one day decided never to tolerate a rider again. A wild horse will usually buck two or three times and then lose heart, although some are genuine rogues that can never be broken. The average age of a bronc is between twelve and fifteen years old, and most of them have been bucking for years. A cowboy learns to recognise a particular horse's bucking routine and tries to adapt his riding accordingly—until he is allotted the horse whose performance is different every time!

Left: saddle bronc riding is timed at eight or ten seconds — easily long enough for a spill like this to happen. **Above:** Steer wrestling. The steer is given a head start and chased by two cowboys . . .

The broncs are in top condition in spite of their rough appearance and so their morale is always high; high enough to feel that they can flatten any would-be rider, and because they perform only for eight or ten seconds at a time they rarely get dispirited. Many are notorious personalities, and at the National Finals, which is to rodeo what Wimbledon is to tennis, there is an award for the Bucking Horse of the Year. There has been a great deal of controversy over the use of the flank, or bucking strap, on the grounds that it is a cruel device. This is simply not true. The flank is lined with sheepskin and is never cinched tight enough to hurt the horse. It tickles, and the bronc will squirm and buck to try and rid himself of it. Although most horses would buck without it, it does contribute to their performance and it makes the animal a more difficult ride.

Seconds in the Saddle

There are five major events in rodeo; saddle bronc riding, bareback riding, bull riding, steer wrestling and calf roping.

In saddle bronc riding, the contest may be timed to either eight or ten seconds. To qualify, the rider must spur the horse over the break of the shoulder when the bronc's front feet hit the ground the first jump out of the chute; he must not lose his stirrup or touch the horse, saddle or rein with his free hand. Bronc riders spur in a raking motion, from the neck to the cantleboard, which requires precision, balance and delicate timing. The saddles are made to rigid Rodeo Cowboys' Association specifications and spurs must have blunt, loose rowels.

11

Equivalent rules apply to the bareback riding, except that the bareback riders roll their spurs up the horse's neck—called 'jerking their knees'—and then throw their feet high and wide. A bareback ride lasts for eight seconds. In both events the performance is judged 50 per cent on the horse and 50 per cent on the rider.

Bull riding is the most dangerous sport of all—a bronc, once he has dislodged his rider, will very rarely turn on him deliberately. A bull has no such inhibitions; the fallen cowboy has to regain his feet and move like greased lightning. The rider does not have to spur; it is as much as he can do to cling on with his permitted hand to the rope, tied loosely around the bull's belly, to which a heavy, clanking bell is attached. The bull riding event calls for the help of two rodeo clowns. These men are only secondarily clowns in the humorous sense; their primary job is to distract the bull from the dismounted cowboy and this needs agility and nerves of steel.

The calf-roping contest requires the utmost co-ordination between horse and rider. A good roping horse, like a good dogging horse used in steer wrestling, is hard to come by and is highly prized. Some cowboys own their own roping and dogging horses and lend them to other competitors, for which they are paid one quarter of the others' winnings. The calf, with a headstart into the arena, trips the automatic barrier and the time starts with a flag. The husky little creature zigzags across, hotly pursued by the cowboy who whirls his lariat around his head and finally throws it. A calf is a remarkably difficult animal to rope, and many a time the lariat either misses it altogether or the calf gallops straight through the loop and out the other side. Once the calf is caught the horse stops instantly and pulls back, keeping the rope taut between calf and saddle horn but not dragging the animal. The cowboy in the meantime is straddling the calf and tying three of its legs together as quickly as he knows how, with the pigging string that he carries in his teeth during the race across the arena. He must tie the calf in a particular way—with three wraps and a 'hooey'—and it must remain tied for six seconds. Sometimes, whilst he is facing the judges with his arms triumphantly raised, the small calf is trotting furiously away in the background, to the great amusement of the crowd . . .

The bulldogging, or steer wrestling event, is also timed. The steer is given a headstart and is pursued by two cowboys, of whom one is the wrestler and the other the hazer who keeps the steer running straight and who gets a cut out of the winnings. As the two horses close up on the racing steer, the bulldogger flings himself sideways off his own horse and on to the steer, grasping its horns. He must bring the steer to a stop and wrestle it to the ground, twisting its head to one side so that it has no option but to fall. All four of its legs must be facing in the same direction for it to constitute a legal fall, and holds of scientific leverage are used to throw the animal, which weighs hundreds of pounds more than the man.

Chuckwagon Thoroughbreds

As well as these main events, there are others such as wild cow milking, wild horse races and the famous chuckwagon racing. In this event, four chuckwagons per heat line up on the track, each drawn by a team of four thoroughbreds, lean and fit as greyhounds, and each flanked by four dismounted outriders. At the starting signal, tent poles and a cooking stove are loaded into each wagon by the outriders. The driver stirs up his team and drives them round a set of barrels so as to execute a figure-of-eight. He then heads his team and wagon for the race-track and sets off on the half-mile gallop for home. The outriders in the meantime are frantically leaping on their excited mounts, often catching up with their respective wagons while they are still horizontal across the saddle. With wild yells they thunder down the track, all the horses straining and sweating, going flat out even when the race is over and the driver is pulling backwards with all his might to stop them.

At the end of the rodeo there is laughter and disappointment; the cowboys sign autographs, drink, gamble or (more usually) pack up quickly and head off to the next rodeo. The sport is in the blood of them all. Tough, highly competitive, it is the most individual sport in

The most famous event in the calendar — the chuckwagon race.

the world, where a few grow rich though most remain poor but determined; where many bones are broken and where some die. But above all it is a sport where a man is free and where he is dependent upon nobody but himself—and the horses he rides . . .

No one can train a horse to buck. He either likes it or he doesn't. All that his owners can do is to give him plenty of rest, feed and water and hope his morale stays high enough that he'll go on trying to flatten every rider who crawls on his back.

A big part of the morale-building is letting the horse think he is winning. That's why the bronc ride in professional rodeos is limited to either eight or ten seconds, depending upon arena conditions.

Bucking horses are at their worst the first twenty jumps from the chute and a cowboy who gets past that first storm should have an odds on chance of riding the bronc from there on out.

Cruel treatment of bucking horses is a myth among misguided animal lovers. Besides being specifically forbidden by a set of rules—written in harmony by the Canadian Rodeo Cowboys Association and the Society for the Prevention of Cruelty to Animals—mistreatment of bucking horses would be a good way for any rodeo stock contractor to commit economic suicide. Under-fed horses simply won't buck at all. (*From the Calgary Exhibition and Stampede Official Programme*)

Twala, aged 22 with owner, writer Frances Pares,
who persuaded him that he was a bronc!

Glossary of Rodeo Terms

Association Saddle—Any saddle built to definite R.C.A. specifications and design and used in saddle bronc riding. It may belong either to the contestant or the rodeo producer.

Barrier—A rope stretched across the front end of the box from which the roper's or steer wrestler's horse comes when the barrier flag drops. According to the arena conditions, the stock is given a pre-determined head start, or score, marked by a scoreline.

Breaking the Barrier—If the contestant rides through or breaks the barrier before it is released a penalty of ten seconds is added to this time.

Hazer—A cowboy who rides along beside a steer, on the opposite side from the steer wrestler, to keep the steer from running away from the steer wrestler's horse.

No Time—When a flag fieldman waves 'No Time' it means that the contestant has not caught or thrown his animal properly and receives no time on that animal in that go-round, but is still entitled to compete in the next go-round.

Pickup Man—A mounted cowboy who helps the rider off a bronc when the ride is completed. The pickup man then removes the flank strap from the bronc and leads the horse out of the arena.

Pigging String—A short piece of soft rope by which a roper ties together the feet of a roped calf or steer.

Pulling Leather—When a bronc rider holds on to the horn, or any part of the saddle, he is said to be pulling leather. Pulling leather disqualifies a saddle bronc rider if it is done before the ride is completed.

Score—The distance between the chute opening and the scoreline, or the amount of head start given to a steer or calf in a roping or steer wrestling event. The length of the score is usually determined by the size of the arena or other local conditions.

Untie Man—An arena employee who, after the flagman has signalled that a tie has qualified, releases the calf or steer from both the rope and the pigging string. Untie men usually work in pairs.

Go-Round—That part of a rodeo that is required to allow each contestant to compete on one head of stock. The number of go-rounds in a rodeo may vary from one in a small one-day contest to as many as seven or more in the larger rodeos.

Re-Rides—Another ride given to a bronc rider or a bull rider in the same go-round when the first ride is unsatisfactory for any of several reasons, such as the horse falling not bucking.

Calgary Stampede definitions

The Spanish Riding School of Vienna

A curious title, one might imagine, for an establishment that is certainly not Spanish, and has such accomplished riders that it could hardly be called a school; but there are good historical reasons for the name . . .

Seven-thirty a.m. is the time to be there. Every morning a traffic cop puts up a hand to the early morning commutors, bringing them to a halt, just outside the ancient Hofburg, between the Michaelerplatz and the Opera House on Vienna's great tree-lined Ringstrasse. It takes some finding, this small corner of old Vienna, but it is worth the trouble. The heavy, pot-bellied houses and solid churches tucked away behind 'tourist' Vienna take one back to the world of Franz-Josef and Johann Strauss, and the quiet of a by-gone age.

As the traffic squeals to a stop the door of the stables opposite one of the entrances to the Hofburg opens, and at a slow walk the fabled white Lipizzaner stallions troop across the road to the main hall to begin their morning work-out. Nobody minds the hold-up, the sight is worth the delay. The light glints on braided uniforms, on polished harness and white flanks, and in a brief moment the files of riders and the most famous horses in the world have disappeared into the oldest riding establishment in existence. And if you couldn't see for the crowd, there's always tomorrow; after all, they've been doing this every day for over 200 years.

What happens in the Riding Hall, the magnificent arena with its tall Corinthian colonnades, its ceiling dripping with chandeliers, its elegant balustraded balconies? Just some very hard work—maybe more sophisticated than that at a normal riding school, but basically done for the same reason—to train the horses into discipline. In this case it is the discipline necessary for them to perform their 'equestrian ballet' which they give at public performances.

Left: the elegant high-stepping trot called the Passage; the Lipizzaner seems to hover just above the ground. **Below:** the School Quadrille, to the music of Bizet. **Right:** a dramatic Courbette, when the horse makes several jumps forward on his hindlegs. The movement is an old battle manœuvre.

The Art of the School

The object of this riding academy is simple to define, if difficult to maintain. It is, to quote the official statement:

To preserve and continue the original principles of Equestrian Art and to demonstrate them in public performance.
To exert a general influence on the art of dressage, based on the classic principles, by training disciples from both Austria and abroad.
And finally to exercise control over the breeding of the Lipizzaner strain by employing as sires only those stallions which have proved their aptitude for Haute École.

In fact the *Spanische Reitschule* of Vienna has preserved these objectives and traditions for 400 years, following the teachings and standard of training set down by the master of them all, Xenophon, who lived in Greece in the Fifth Century B.C.

So to the show. The sunlight lies in chequerboard squares on the combed sand surface of the great hall in the Imperial Palace, the Hofburg.

Opposite the main entrance the Imperial Box is backed by a portrait of the founder, the Emperor Charles VI, whom all riders salute upon their entrance. Under the royal box, in a ground-level enclosure, the distinguished visitors sit—many of whom are more than a little surprised when, as tradition demands, the riders canter into the enclosure and circle around them.

Then the dazzling exhibition of haute école starts. Riders line up in file, slowly doff their bicorn hats, hold their arm out in elegant salute and replace their head-gear. The brown tail-coats, white breeches and silver spurs blend into multicolour spectacle in this great lofty hall as the riders wheel into the first movement.

One may see the *airs and movements* of the haute école in a quadrille of the School; four riders and horses working in perfect unison, each blended into what looks like a single living unit.

Here are some of the movements of the classical school, performed by horses trained according to the principles of classical equitation: work on the long rein; riders of the Grand Quadrille, led by Colonel Hans Handler, Director of the School, in a half-traverse towards the centre; a capriole, and work in the pillars.

No signals from rider to horse—not even the smallest twitch of rein or spur—can be seen as they walk, trot, circle, change leg, led by the Director, Colonel Hans Handler. *Piaffe, Passade* and *Pirouette* are executed in perfect time to a light Viennese musical confection. And these are just the basic steps of the School.

Said Austrian poet Otto Stoessl, of a past performance:

Three or four pairs ride into the lofty wide hall to the sound of trumpet flourishes. Each rider and horse are a team, each horse is unique, a creature that cannot be reproduced, a genius of its species, beautiful and perfect beyond description. The rider in his saddle, the man who governs and directs the horse is, on the other hand, merely a human being like any other. Despite his skill and power, he is quite insignificant in this battle with an elemental force.

That could be putting rather too much stress on the ability of the horse and too little on that of the trainer and rider, but it is an impressive illustration of how the skill and beauty of these horses gets through to the audience.

After the airs, the *Pas de Deux*, a dance in twos. And indeed it *is* a dance, executed by the stallions under the riders. As the School programme says:

. . . a ritual full of verve and of perfection, betraying nothing of the hard work, the tremendous training that went before.

The figures of the dance seem to be moves made on the spur of the moment, never pre-meditated, as they delicately mirror-image each other in precise rhythm to the music of Mozart.

Then, perhaps, there are exercises on the short hand rein between the pillars—the two pillars that take up the centre of the arena—where the horse performs stationary manoeuvres to prove that he can accomplish all the tricky moves that are demanded of him without a rider on his back to direct his action.

Here the horse may carry out a *Piaffe* (a trot without moving forward, with haunches deeply bent) and other movements that, in training, disclose to which of the haute école airs he will best adapt. Only the natural talents of the Lipizzaners are exploited in the School, and artificial movements such as those seen at the circus are frowned on here. Some of the above the ground manoeuvres of the school have their roots in the natural playfulness of young stallions, others in the ancient arts of battle.

High-Point

So follow the *School Springs*, or the *Schools Above the Ground*. Only the really gifted stallions, those with strength and talent and intelligence, are used for these. In this part of the performance the horse either lifts his forehand off the ground or performs a spring, and the airs are divided into the:

Levade Here the horse raises his forehand, draws up his forelegs in a bent position, and rests on his hindlegs with the hocks sharply bent. A sort of temporary defiance of gravity. Stirrups are not used for the Schools above the Ground.

In the *Courbette* one can sniff the odour of war. This movement stems from the battlefields when a mounted knight would jerk up his horse in a fierce panicky type of exaggerated Levade and make him spring forward on his hindlegs, in a desperate attempt to break through the surrounding enemy foot soldiers.

And lastly the *Capriole*, the most difficult of the springs. Only the finest Lipizzaner performs this astonishing lightning spring above the ground. A mixture of high spirits, when young horses like to leap and kick, and the manoeuvres of long ago wars when horsemen would try to leap over their foes, the Capriole has developed into the one movement that most of us imagine would be impossible to a heavy animal.

Unmounted, this enormous spring is dramatic enough, mounted, it shows that Otto Stoessl was not entirely correct when he described the riders of the Spanish School. The movement is in effect a gigantic spring into the air, with the stallion flinging out a violent kick with his hindlegs at the peak moment.

After the School Springs the Quadrille, a ballet of eight or twelve white stallions, allows the audience's temperature to subside. Here the performance recalls the traditional *Karussells* of the past. The Quadrille demands the greatest concentration from riders and horses as they swing through circles and crosses and figures-of-eight to Bizet and Chopin from the band . . .

Six stallion dynasties form the basis of the School's Lipizzaner strain, and all horses bear the name of their ancient sire, Pluto, Conversano, Neapolitano, Favory, Maestoso or Siglavy, and their dam.

The Lipizzaners

They came originally from Spain and, though centuries have passed, their aptitude for high school training has been nurtured carefully. These chief actors of the Spanish School of Vienna are the last descendants of horses that were known as far back as the days of the Roman Caesars; then they were used for chariot races, triumphal processions and military campaigns. From Rome and Carthage they were later sent to the Spanish colonies.

Lipizzaners from Spain were taken to Austria in 1562 when Archduke Karl built a stable in Lipizza near Trieste. From there they were selected and the best used for the Spanish Riding School of Vienna, first recorded as a riding establishment about ten years later.

The rough countryside with its sparse growth of grass soon toughened these horses, who had been used to mild climates and lush vegetation. They gained stamina, courage, perseverance. For some time the strain was kept absolutely pure, then Italian, Danish and German blood was introduced.

Today the stock of Lipizzaners numbers around 60 stallions at the Riding School and about 40 mares and 80 young at the stud, now at Piber in the Styria region of Austria. Just six stallion dynasties form the basis of the strain; they can be traced back like this:

Pluto	(White)	Born 1765	originally Danish
Conversano	(Black)	Born 1767	originally Neapolitan
Neapolitano	(Bay)	Born 1790	originally Neapolitan
Favory	(Dun)	Born 1779	originally Lipizzaner
Maestoso	(White)	Born 1819	{ originally Lipizzaner (father) / originally Spanish (mother)
Siglavy	(White)	Born 1810	originally Arab

Left: only about half the young stallions bred at Piber pass their school entry test: the rest are sold. This one is used for circus work. Above, outdoor exercise at Vienna, and right, riders doff their hats in salute to their founder, Emperor Charles VI.

Long ago various colours were used by the School, but now whites are always crossed with whites so that today the white horse is always associated with the School. The stallions are all known by one of the names of their ancient sires, coupled with the name of their dam.

The foals, however, are certainly not born white—anything from mouse to black—and develop their snow-white coats around their seventh year. They roam free at the Piber stud until their fourth autumn, when a dozen young stallions are taken to Vienna to commence their long training. Only half of them pass the first test, the others are sold. Those that come on the open market are sought out by keen riders and schools, for their fine character and intelligence makes them suitable for a hundred different roles.

The young stallions that are kept by the School have the hardest time. That chorus-girl lightness and military precision does not come in a month, or a year—or even four years. It takes five long patient years for them to mature in the classical skills. They have just 45 minutes training a day—not long perhaps, but these horses must never leave their training tired or poor-tempered. It would be a mistake to hurry the art that the intelligent Lipizzaners learn so well and perform so elegantly.

And so, after their years of training, after stern and constant discipline, Pluto Nautika or Favory Basilica will appear with the others in the regular Sunday high-school performance in the great Riding Hall at the Hofburg, demonstrating the arts that Xenophon taught twenty-five centuries ago; the same skills that have been on display at the Spanish Riding School of Vienna for 400 years.

The Spanish Riding School occasionally travels outside the confines of Vienna's Hofburg. Here they are at Wembley, in London.

The U.S. Army Rescues the Lipizzaners

In 1945 Vienna was subjected to Allied bombing attacks and the white stallions were in danger. The school was shut down and the Lipizzaners smuggled, against the orders of the Nazi occupiers, by Colonel Alois Podhajsky the chief of the academy, to a country town 200 miles away. During that hazardous trip the train was gunned and bombed. *The horses*, says the Colonel, *were the calmest of us all. They had discipline and dignity.* In St. Martin they were stabled on an estate which was desperate for food, until the arrival of the U.S. Army under the command of General Paton. When he heard about the plight of the famed Lipizzaners, Paton, who had ridden with Podhajsky in the Olympic Games, ordered an haute école show for the visiting U.S. Under-Secretary of War. Podhajsky took the opportunity (as Paton had arranged) to plead his cause—and the horses were made wards of the U.S. Army until peace was restored. Paton even ordered a task force to go into still-occupied Czechoslovakia to fetch out the Lipizzaner mares and foals so that the future of the great line was safe . . .

The Great American Quarter Horse

First question is, of course, a quarter of what? The name of this versatile horse has nothing to do with breeding—it isn't a quarter-anything, and it has nothing to do with its anatomy.

It began long ago when Virginia was forested country, and the early settlers, when they had a little time for anything other than dawn-to-dusk work on the land, cut tracks into the forest and used them for short races—mostly around a quarter-mile in length. The horses they used —and later bred—for this sport, were fast starters and fast movers over this distance. Hence the name.

Janus, a thoroughbred of the time, sired the original Quarter Horses, and now their quick responses to weight, balance and rein makes them ideal for a hundred purposes . . .

Little did those settlers know, 300 years ago, that they were developing the breed of horse that would eventually become part of the leisure lives of more riders than any other horse in the country. For today the American Quarter Horse Association, formed in 1940, has on its register no less than 700,000 horses and 55,000 members spread over the four corners of the globe.

Why this tremendous popularity? The last two decades have seen the rapid rise of equestrian sports and pastimes, from show jumping competitions to pony trekking. In the United States one of the few animals that can adapt and excel in almost the entire range of riding activities is the Quarter Horse.

Cutting horse, calf or steer roping horse, working cow-horse, the American Quarter Horse is the most versatile of them all.

Used as a jumper the Quarter Horse is willing and eager to clear fences, and as a hunter he is a comfortable ride, and happily clears barriers that confront horse and rider on cross-country terrain. As a polo pony he is really great—fine at quick starting, stopping, backing, and balanced at all speeds.

At Western pleasure classes he demonstrates walk, trot and canter in an unruffled way and can show his change of gait with the best. And in the 'English Pleasure' class, a recent addition to U.S. competitive events, he seems equally happy under English tack with full bridle or curb bit, and when judged in this class for conformation, manners and presence, the Quarter Horse has little to fear.

Are there other roles for this versatile animal? There are dozens. He is a great performer at barrel-racing, which calls for speed and agility. As a cutting horse he knows no peer—the Quarter Horse's 'cow-sense' is a characteristic that made him famous from way back, as a working cow-horse.

The Quarter Horse, in native habitat.

Barrel racing calls for speed and agility **(left)** and Western Pleasure for the right temperament — the Quarter horse is popular for both.

For gymkhana work he is as enthusiastic as his young riders, and in bending races, particularly, he comes into his own.

Rodeo riders, especially professionals whose incomes are measured by their skill at roping and bull-dogging competitions, have long ago learned that this is the horse to carry them to success. With his speed and lighting responses, plus dependability, he is unbeatable. And as a bonus his placid temperament helps him—and his rider—to keep cool in the noise and bustle of crowded meetings.

The Perfect Quarter Horse

Below is the American Quarter Horse Association's list of Conformation Standards for the Quarter Horse. The enjoyment of most things is in direct ratio to our understanding of them, and this certainly applies to appreciating horses. Try to remember some of the points below—you never know when you may be able to surprise an expert with your knowledge . . .

Head:

The head of a Quarter Horse reflects alert intelligence. This is due to his short, broad head, topped by little 'fox ears' and by his wide-set, kind eyes and large, sensitive nostrils, short muzzle and firm mouth. Well developed jaws give the impression of great strength.

Neck:

The head of the Quarter Horse joins the neck at a near forty-five degree angle, with a distinct space between jaw-bone and neck muscles, to allow him to work with his head down and not restrict his breathing. The medium length, slightly arched, full neck blends into sloping shoulders.

Shoulders:

The Quarter Horse's unusually good saddle back is created by his medium-high but sharp withers, extending well-back and combining with his deep sloping shoulders, so that the saddle is held in proper position for balanced action.

... at grass, and at work.

Chest and Forelegs:
The Quarter Horse is deep and broad chested, as indicated by his great heart girth and wide-set forelegs which blend into his shoulders. The smooth joints and very short cannons are set on clean fetlocks and the medium length pasterns are supported by sound feet. The powerfully muscled forearm tapers to the knee, whether viewed from the front or back.

Back:
The short saddle back of the Quarter Horse is characterised by being close coupled and especially full and powerful across the kidney. The barrel is formed by deep, well-sprung ribs back to the hip joints, and the under line comes back straight to the flank.

Rear Quarters:
The rear quarters are broad, deep, and heavy, viewed from either side or rear, and are muscled so they are full through the thigh, stifle, gaskin and down to the hock. The hind leg is muscled inside and out, the whole indicating the great driving power the Quarter Horse possesses. When viewed from the rear there is great width, extending evenly from top of thigh to bottom of the stifle and gaskin. The hocks are wide, deep, straight and clean.

Bones, Legs and Feet:
The flat, clean, flinty bones are free from fleshiness and puffs but still show much substance. The foot should be well-rounded and roomy, with an especially deep open heel.

Stance:
The Quarter Horse normally stands perfectly at ease with his legs well under him; this explains his ability to move quickly in any direction.

Action:
The Quarter Horse is uniquely collected in his action and turns or stops with noticeable ease and balance, with his hocks always well under him.

It's a long time now since those early American pioneers started to race a horse whose foundation went back to Arab, Barb and Turk breeds brought to North America by Spanish explorers in the 15th Century. It's a long time since settlers moved over the country and took their Quarter Horse with them to help conquer and tame the land around them. But the Quarter Horse is still with us—and in greater numbers than ever—one of the most versatile horses the world has known.

Show Jumping—The Universal Sport

Next to jump, Fiorello, ridden by Captain Raimondo d'Inzeo from Italy.
The address system echoes out over the packed darkness surrounding the arena. A massive chestnut trots out of the collecting ring into the television lights and the solitude of the jumping ring. In front of the main box d'Inzeo stops, salutes. The starting bell rings and, tracked by two cameras, the horse is wheeled round to face the approach to the first jump. A typical international show jumping class is about to begin . . .

It all started where most horse-and-riding innovations started—in the English countryside, way back in 1709. This was the year that an Act of Parliament, called the Enclosure Act, was passed, and it marked the changeover in England from what was basically communal village agriculture to privately-owned parcels of land. Designed to increase food production for the population-explosion of the time, it changed the face of Britain.

The Enclosure Act also posed some thorny problems for the landed gentry of the day. Their hunting activities had, up to this point, been over open heaths and commons, unfenced, unhedged. Suddenly this open land sprouted gates, hedges and other obstacles in the formerly uninterrupted hunting scene.

Show Jumping — the Universal Sport
Show jumping has competitions to suit all grades of horse and rider. **Below** is international rider Anneli Drummond-Hay clearing a fence at Hickstead, England, and the colour shot is of a young horsewoman at a local show.

Except in battle, horses—and riders for that matter—had previously had very little occasion to leave the ground dramatically, but with these new obstacles it was jump or stay at home. And so the hunting fanatics of the 18th Century put their horses at the fences—and were pleasantly surprised to find that their steeds not only liked the new game, but jumped naturally and well.

Show jumping officially began in 1866 at a harness show in Paris, France, when a class was arranged for a few horses with jumping qualities. As most of the actual jumping was done over the local countryside the competition attracted very few of the spectators attending the show.

In 1900, an entry in the Olympic Games records shows that three jumping classes took place—Prize jumping (whatever that was), High Jumping and, surprisingly, Long Jumping. But the sport only became recognisable in the 1912 Olympiad when there were individual and team events, won by Sweden and France. The United States had to wait until the Los Angeles Olympics in 1932 to appear in the winners' lists, and Great Britain, mother country of modern equestrian sport, until 1948.

In 1912, show jumping ran under loose rules, and as far as can be gathered, every rider made up his own as he jumped. This led to the formation of the F.E.I. (Fédération Equestre Internationale) so that all riders in show jumping classes from Durban to Detroit would know exactly how many penalty points they collected, and for what faults.

Left: a junior rider clears a very senior fence. **Top:** Pat Smythe in her show jumping days was undoubtedly the most famous rider in the world. Clearing the wall is Alan Oliver, one of Britain's top riders.

In Britain the sport grew slowly until in the Twenties it formed part of most agricultural shows. Jumps were flimsy and jumpers were few—mostly country riders, with a sprinkling of military riders seen only at shows such as the Royal Tournament. And if, at these early shows, there was a gap in the general entertainment, the show jumping judges would often suggest that the riders go over the whole course a second time!

It was World War II that proved the watershed for the sport, coupled with the development of television.

By the 1950's the sport was spreading from the important international shows to 'Saturday Gymkhanas' held in farmers' fields in the provinces of France, Germany, Britain and, to a lesser degree, the United States. But it took some years before the governing bodies learned that show jumping was not a sport just for the rich, and only recently has prize money in various forms risen to amounts more related to the real cost in effort and cash of maintaining suitable horses.

Widening popularity soon boosted the sport to higher levels and international competition sharpened the skill of riders from a score of 'riding' countries. The rules of show jumping were relatively simple, at least in essence, and everyone, from devoted teenage riders to television addicts could understand what it was all about. A fence down was a fence down—and everyone knew that meant four penalty points against the horse-and-rider. The build-up of tension as horse after horse went through a clear or penalised round ensured increasing attention from spectators at ringside and television set alike. Riders and horses at the top of the sport became household names. In Europe, at least, show jumping was on the crest of a wave, and still is . . .

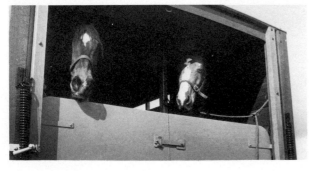

Show jumping has spread in popularity throughout the world. Here a girl takes a big upright at a riding centre in California. **Opposite page, top:** Germany's Alwin Schockemöhle, and **lower right,** his rival and friend, Harvey Smith.

In the United States show jumping is a fast-growing sport. Since the introduction of many riding centres in new communities, regional shows are in vogue, and more national-calibre tests are on the way.

To the vast majority of fans a television screen is the closest to a horse show they'll ever get. But that doesn't stop them being experts. The finer points of show jumping are the ones to put you in that category, and although the basic F.E.I. rules are simple, here are a few reminders of the way show jumping is organised . . .

Types of Competition

The simplest type of competition (or 'class' as most European riders call it) is one in which the speed of a round has little bearing. Each horse and rider jumps a set number of fences (in the right order, or disqualification results) and if several have collected an equal number of faults (four for a knock-down or a foot in the water-jump, three for various disobediences, etc.) or none at all—a further round (a jump-off) is jumped.

Then there is the speed event, when riders really push their horses hard around the course in an all-out effort to clip off the split-seconds. Each fence knocked down may have a five or six-second penalty score. But probably the most dramatic of all is the *puissance* event, in which height is the important factor. Usually there are just a few fences, and as the competitors are reduced in number, the fences are slowly raised inch by agonising inch, until there may be just one fence left, at a towering 7 feet.

Yorkshireman Harvey Smith takes a spread at Badminton, and **below,** World Champion David Broome clears a fence on a novice horse. Style is not important in show jumping — just get over the fence clear! **Opposite** you see a horse at a South African show that didn't, and **far right,** one that usually did (it's British Olympic medallist Marion Mould and Stroller). David Broome smiles for the camera, and a newcomer tries her first jump.

There are many other types of competition which can be seen at smaller shows—contests of skill, riding, jumping, speed and agility—Fault-and-Out events, Take-Your-Own-Line competitions, Scurry, Pair Relays and so on.

They can all be readily understood by the watching spectators, which is part of the universal fascination of the sport. There are no points for style. You can look like a *bereiter* from the Spanish School of Vienna or a sack of corn—if you clear that fence you don't get penalised.

Fences

They are of two kinds, upright and spread. Uprights, considered to be the more difficult of the two types, are designed to test the horse's high-jumping capabilities, and the spread his height-plus-length prowess. The trouble with the upright (from the horse's point of view) is that the ground-line, the base of the jump on the approach side, is right under the fence itself. Now a horse likes his ground-line to be forward of the fence so that he can shoot a quick glance at it and judge the distance he needs to stand back for the correct take-off distance. The ground-line of the upright fence tends to bring him in too close for comfort. This is where the expert watcher pays close attention to the rider's actions and judges his skill at shortening or lengthening his mount's pace to the correct take-off point. In theory, by the way, the horse jumps in a perfect arc, the radius of which is the height of the upright jump itself. That's theory: in practice the arc often gets a bit dented.

Examples of upright, or straight, fences are a five-bar or ornamental gate, a wall, post and rails, single rail. They are usually no more than 4 ft 9 ins. high, except for championship classes, in which they may be up to 5 ft 6 ins.

Spread fences—those with width as well as height—are double oxers, triple bars, hog's backs, parallel bars and, of course, water jumps. These last vary from 12 ft to 16 ft long and generally have a small brush hedge about 2 ft high on the take-off side of the water itself. Two or three fences are sometimes placed near each other (not more than 13 yards apart) and are collectively called a combination jump. The distance between them depends on how many strides the horse is expected to take from one to the other. A stride is about eight to nine feet at a canter, and as often as not the distance between two fences will be 24 ft, necessitating several adjustments of stride through the combination. This is undoubtedly the toughest test of the lot in the show jumping arena, and has been the downfall of most riders at some critical point in their career.

The route of the course itself is not as simple as it looks when you watch an accomplished rider sail through to a clear round. Usually a course will be between 550 to 950 yards long and be designed to promote good jumping rather than to fool the rider and horse with trick jumps or difficult turns, although some jumps *will* be placed to test the control of horse and rider—perhaps a straight jump following water (which needs speed to cover successfully) and at a sharp angle to it. Course-building is a carefully acquired skill and those who can lay out a successful course are in great international demand.

Horses

No specific breed of horse is the one-and-only for this sport. Some of the most successful jumpers have been of humble pedigree: some have been 17 to 18 hands high monsters (the famous Vibart was 17 h.h. and Harvey Smith's Ten-to-Twelve is a massive 18·1½ h.h.) and some have been little more than ponies—like Marion Mould's Stroller who at 14·2 h.h. took his rider to world championship and an Olympic medal.

The right temperament, with a little fire, is ideal. Height is, curiously, not of supreme importance, except in puissance events. The most vital area is the horse's quarters and hocks, for this is where all the motive power, the impulsion, comes from. The ability to jump runs right through the range of equines and almost all (except perhaps the Shetland at one end and the Shire at the other!) may have show jumping potential. Why not try your own pony on a home-built course sometime . . .

Judging—the International Rules

Those competitions not primarily concerned with speed are judged under 'Table A' in which faults, or penalty points, are given like this:

Fence knocked down with fore or hind legs   4 faults
Disobediences: 1st   3 faults
(cumulative)
                 2nd   6 faults
                 3rd   elimination
Falls: horse or rider or both   8 faults
Time: exceeding the 'time allowed' (the time in which it is estimated a horse should easily complete the course): for each second over: $\frac{1}{4}$ fault

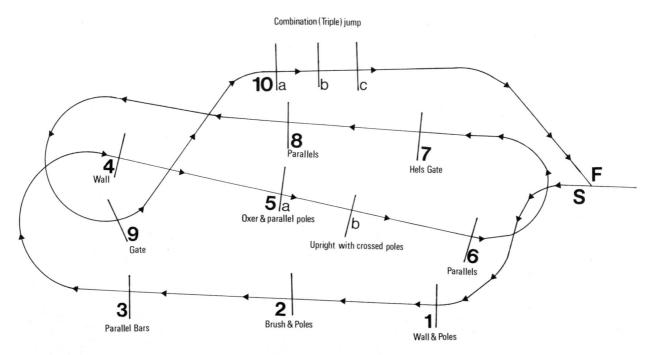

Typical Jumping Course

Arabian Horses of Jordan and Persia

When the summer temperature soared to sweltering heights down by the Dead Sea, the horses of the Royal Jordanian Stud would be enjoying the cooler air of Amman. For the rest of the year they were kept at Shune, an estate east of the River Jordan where King Hussein had a 'leisure house'.

Those were the halcyon years, when the horses were still at Shune before the sad and disruptive Arab-Israeli war. The conflict brought fighting swiftly to Jericho, only a few miles away, and when word came to the stables that there had been shooting at a nearby stud, the King's Horsemaster decided on action. Horses were saddled for him, his wife, Rahdi the stud groom and for the half-dozen other Bedouin who remained out of a normal complement of thirty grooms. Between them they led as many of the animals as they could manage and the remainder—stallions, young stock, mares and foals, were turned loose to follow, as they trekked off into the darkness of pre-dawn, making for Amman.

For safety they kept clear of the road that snakes down from the capital to Jericho, and rode across country, the horses picking their way through stony wadis, across boulder-strewn tracks and up precipitous slopes covered in loose shale. It took them twelve hours to make the 70 kilometre haul up to Amman, yet when they arrived many of the animals were still bucking and playing around as though they had just left their stable. But that is only one small illustration, amongst thousands, of the exceptional stamina and courage of the most beautiful breed of horses in the world . . .

There are many splendid studs of Arabian horses in countries outside the Middle East—in America, England and Poland to name a few; but in Arab eyes only those horses whose lineage springs from one of the few priceless blood-lines that are said to trace back at least as far as the sixth century, can be considered truly *asil*, that is, pure bred.

Jordan's Royal Stud

For hundreds of years a small stock of horses, in a relatively small area, were kept fanatically pure bred by breeding only from the most intelligent, beautiful and speedy of the young stock. The arduous environment helped by killing off the less hardy, and this culling that continued for generation after generation resulted in the preservation of those few blood-lines of superb horses. When the Arabs went to war their stallions mated with horses of other breeds, but no alien horse was ever taken back to sully the lovely Arabian stock.

However, the fame of the desert Arabs of the Near and Middle East brought many buyers from other lands, gradually the best of the stallions were regularly exported, and only a few mares of the most prized strains were retained. More recently the Bedouin, the traditional horse-breeders, in dire need of the small sum a foal will fetch whatever its parentage, have been less meticulous in their choice of a stallion, and now there are few truly *asil* horses in the part of the world that produced them.

The Royal Jordanian Stud was started less than twenty years ago to preserve and establish the blood of the few horses of ancient lineage that remained. Jordan is not a rich country and there were no vast sums to expend on the project, but there was a nucleus of *asil* mares that had belonged to King Hussein's grandfather, and gradually other horses of equally indis-

Left: Iran's Imperial Guard in the ceremonial dress worn at their Shah's coronation.

Above: The Jordan Royal Stud, before the Six-Day war.

putable pure breeding were found. Some were discovered on the race-course at Beirut, some came from the tents of sheikhs far out in the desert; one mare was seen working a Bedouin plough, another came from the ranks of the police force. Slowly the stock was built up and bred from and now the stud in Jordan, housed in dazzling white Moorish style stabling on the outskirts of Amman, is renowned for breeding some of the finest desert Arabian horses in the Middle East, and in the world.

Horses of the Shah

Iran has been a land of horses for more than 3,000 years, and although the country, spurred by the Shah's 'white revolution' of reform, is thrusting with fantastic speed into modernity, in many parts of that vast area horses must remain a necessary part of every-day life for some time to come. But in other parts horses have been superceded so rapidly by mechanisation, that a Royal Horse Society of Iran has been formed to try and preserve a great heritage.

The Shah himself is a fine horseman and this new interest in the Persian horse breeds, and in general equitation, radiates mainly from the Royal Horsemaster, and the Imperial Stud, at Farahabad outside Tehran. Many magnificent Persian horses of different types are kept at the royal stables—some of them the Shah's favourite stallions that he rides amongst the rocky, difficult terrain of his hunting preserves—and Persian Arabs, taller animals than the desert Arabian and without the characteristic 'dished' face, but with much of the same beauty and fire. Two thoroughbreds from Britain have recently been imported, and these, crossed with Jadran Arab and Plateau Persian are being used to develop a new type called, after the Shah, Pahlavan.

Some of the best horses at Farahabad are Turkoman. The Turkoman peoples live south-east of the Caspian Sea and are said to be descendants of the hordes of Genghis Khan, the Mongol conqueror who ravaged Iran during the 13th century. For hundreds of years the Turkoman tribes were nomadic horse-breeders, but under the Shah's agricultural reforms they are now almost all settled, prosperous farmers, raising sheep and camels and cropping the steppe-land where they live with wheat and barley. Some herds of semi-wild Turkoman mares still roam the sara, but the cherished stallion once tethered outside each yurt, or house, is yearly becoming a rarer sight. These horses are eminently suited to their arid environment, with the stamina that allows them to do 100 miles in a day without effort. In 1935 the first three horses home in a 4,300 kilometre race from Eshkabad on the Iranian frontier to Moscow, were Turkoman. They took 84 days, three at a stretch over waterless desert, and covered the last 500 metres at a gallop!

Below: the Italian ambassador to Iran and his horse, 1966. He had been given this stallion, had trained him to perfection — and had never used a bit. They always bowed to each other like this before the day's work!

Right: a Turkoman from Iran and his horse. A native of country similar to the Russian Steppes, the Turkoman puts seven layers of felt on his mount as insulation against temperature changes.

Nowadays not all the Turkoman ride in from the desert for the annual tribal races, they arrive in trucks and lorries and shiny cars, but the younger (and thus the lightest) sons of the racing families still take part as jockeys, both in the north-east and down on the more sophisticated course outside Tehran. And the Turkoman horses they ride with such success remain the fine-drawn creatures they have always been, kept in condition by a method that goes back centuries. This consists of layers of felt, sometimes as many as eight, that the horse wears from the time he is first tethered and hand-fed—mostly with protein—at the age of eighteen months, except for a daily twenty-minute 'airing of the horse', and when racing. The rugs insulate the animal against the heat of summer and the winter's cold and, when it is being ridden, sweat off the smallest sign of fat.

Show Jumping Comes to Iran

Apart from the Turkoman the only other racing interests in Iran are centred round some of the oilfields in the south, but the Royal Horse Society is hoping to revive general interest in the sport. Gymkhanas and other events are beginning to catch on and a show jumping competition, staged at the Imperial Stud and attended by the Shah and the Empress and televised to thousands of Persians, has put this form of equitation well to the fore. It also receives enthusiastic support from the cavalry sections of the Imperial Guard, whose Commanding Officer learned his riding at the famous French school of Saumur where he become one of the élite Cadre Noir.

One of the main objectives of the Royal Horse Society is to encourage the breeding of Persian and some non-Persian horses, and to register the various breeds. This will not be such a very difficult task with Turkoman horses, but must take many years when it comes to types like the Plateau Persian; a horse bred by the tribes that roam vast areas of the middle and south Zagros mountains.

One of the most interesting breeds to register must be the Caspian—which in fact already has its own stud book, compiled by the American wife of a Persian, who re-discovered and developed this ancient line of miniature horses. They are very rare, perhaps only fifty specimens in all Iran, and Mrs. Firouz found the nucleus for her stud near Tehran, pulling heavy loads through the narrow streets, or carrying packs round the twisting alleys of bazaars. These little creatures are not ponies, and much research has established that they may well be direct descendants of the tiny horses that roamed the Zagros mountains in prehistoric times. They range in height from 9 h.h. to 11·2, have the kind of bone structure that allows them to move fast over rough ground, and possess very kind temperaments. The Caspian Stud book is now recognised in both Britain and America, and some of the miniature horses are already in the States.

In some Middle Eastern countries horses are almost a thing of the past, lost in the noise and hustle of a mechanical age, and it is good to know that a vast country like Iran, and a small one like Jordan, alike have the wisdom to preserve this equine heritage.

Top: exercising Jordan's Royal horses and **left,** exercising Iran's Royal Grooms! **Above:** at seven months, a perfect example of a young Arabian filly — she is from an ancient, almost-lost bloodline.

British Native Ponies . . . English Breeds

Well, what *is* the difference between a horse and a pony? That's the first question most people ask when they see a pony. Officially, the answer is that a fully-grown pony is no taller at the withers (top of the shoulders) than 14·2 hands high. Each hand, by the way, measures 4 inches, which is about the width of a grown man's hand. A pony that is 14·2 h.h. is in fact 58 inches high.

All breeds of English, Scottish, Welsh and Irish mountain and moorland ponies are named after the districts from which they come—and, as may be seen from a glance at the map on page 55, all these areas are exposed to extreme weather conditions, with the exception of the New Forest.

These pony 'tribes' have lived for generations on mountains and moorlands, without shelter, and without food other than the natural herbage of the district, which was often sparse, particularly in winter. Climate and diet bred, over the years, the true pony, as nothing of greater size could be reared in such conditions. The rigours of their lives, and those of their ancestors, bred animals often sturdier than their larger counterpart, the horse.

Britain's native ponies have had to earn their living over the centuries, whether it was in the discomfort of working underground, hauling coal from the pit face to the surface (which was the use to which many of the smaller breeds able to negotiate the low galleries were put), or in the blazing heat of India where many were sent to help the Army carry its equipment over the rough terrain.

A CONVINCING TEST.
Youth (on Pony). "COME ON, GRAN'PA! IT'S SAFE ENOUGH. BORE US EASILY!"

Three handsome Exmoor ponies, and **left,** a comment from the rider of what looks like a Shetland — from *Punch,* 1896.

Each of the breeds now has its own society, formed to preserve the breed, and to lay down certain standards up to which animals have to measure in order to be considered true representatives of their breed.

The pony today is probably more popular in the British Isles than it has ever been, for since the last war there has been a tremendous up-surge in all types of equestrian sports, and the pony is the ideal animal on which a child may start.

Probably the best opportunity of seeing native ponies today is at the *Ponies of Britain Show*, an annual two-day concourse where all the breeds of native ponies assemble.

Another fine sight, to be seen at many of the leading horse shows in the country, is a meet of the British Driving Society (no, not a gathering of the latest automobiles!) in which most of the pony breeds are represented, driving 19th Century traps and other vehicles.

The nine mountain-and-moorland breeds described in various sections of this book are the only ones which remain in Britain today, and although when travelling through the country it is possible to see the native mountain-and-moorland ponies roaming freely in some areas, they are no longer truly wild. All belong to someone, and are turned out in the forest or on the moor for cheap grazing, each pony being branded or marked by its owner.

Looking at the map, which shows the native regions of the surviving breeds of England's ponies, you'll see that the breeds come from the countryside bordering the sea in the south—Dartmoor, Exmoor and New Forest ponies—and in the north the two surviving breeds, the Dales and the Fell, come from hill-country. The reason for this is that Britain is densely populated, and as land has been taken for development, the centre of the country has become urbanised, originally because of the location of the coal mines. Other land has been cultivated by farmers to produce home-grown food, of which Britain is perpetually short.

In view of this development, both industrial and agricultural, plus the usual series of population explosions, Britons (at least those interested in ponies) are indeed lucky that five English, two Scottish, one Irish and a Welsh breed, are still able to exist under natural conditions.

Ponies on Dartmoor in February.

46

English Breeds

Here, briefly, are the various backgrounds of the English breeds, each with its official breed society's description.

Dales

Up in the north east of England, before the development of the automobile, the Dales pony was the 'Model T' of the day, used by the butcher, baker, coalman, grocer and milkman to deliver their goods. Still earlier, the Dales pony had been used to haul coal and lead from the mines to factories or docks. Today, in this age of leisure activities, the Dales makes a pleasant riding pony.

During the last century the War Department in Britain found these ponies to be so hardy and adaptable that large numbers were purchased and sent from their cold, bleak moors and dales to the contrasting heat of India. They survived—even thrived—both on the hot plains and in the dizzy heights of the mountains, and in many cases they proved far more adaptable to extreme conditions than their masters. In fact the War Department was so impressed with their performance that subsidies were given to promote their breeding.

The Dales pony is the largest in size of the native breeds of pony in Britain. To increase its size it was crossed extensively with its big cousin the Clydesdale, one of the draught-horse breeds from much the same area. In fact due to this cross-breeding, the Dales pony has become heavier in appearance and has tended to lose some of the characteristics familiar to ponies, although it retains the pony-type head.

Above: a sturdy Dales pony. **Right:** "I don't care what kind of pony you are, you're all mine!"

Breed Description

Height: 14 h.h. to a maximum of 14·2 h.h.

Colours: Predominantly black, dark brown and grey. White markings are permitted in the shape of the star on the face, snip on the nose and on the hind coronets only. Piebalds and skewbalds are not allowed.

Head: Small, neat, with well spaced, small, neat ears, slightly incurving.

Neck: Elegant and well arched from well-laid sloping shoulders.

Back: Short and strong, well ribbed and deep, with ample heart room.

Hind-quarters: Strong, the tail set well on, with good second thigh.

Limbs: At each corner of clean, flat flinty bone, below good flat knees, strong forearms and clean-cut hocks.

Feet: Hard, blue feet, developed to counter the rough terrain where the ponies have been bred. Fetlocks should be sloping with good feathering on the heels.

Action: The walk, using every joint, should be brisk and keen. The trot should be high, clean and true, moving off all four legs.

Dales pony at a National show in England.

Dartmoor

Dartmoor is a bleak, lonely part of the south west of England, a region which often gets the worst of the weather, with frequent rain and snow, and more often than not it is shrouded in mist and fog. To live in this atmosphere with its miles of uncultivated bracken and rough grassland, a pony has to be strong and hardy.

In centuries past Dartmoor ponies roamed the moor in wild herds. As they became more domesticated, different breeds of ponies were introduced to be crossed with them. The sad result was that these 'imported' ponies were not able to stand the extreme weather, and some very weak and poor animals were produced. The breed very nearly became extinct.

Later a number of these cross-bred ponies were exported to the United States and Canada as being true representatives of the breed. The Dartmoor Pony Society had to do a great deal of work to re-introduce the true breed. Indeed the Society, formed in 1920, was probably

just in time to save the breed from total extinction, as during World War I troops had been stationed on the moor and had used the ponies to supplement their rations!

Many of the ponies on the moor today are used for trekking, a sport which has appealed to many people in recent years as a relaxing vacation which includes a little light exercise, combined with some leisurely country tours.

Breed Description

Height: Not exceeding 12·2 h.h.

Colour: Preferably bay, black or brown, but there is no colour bar except for skewbalds and piebalds. Excessive white with any colour is not encouraged.

Head: The head should be small, well set on and blood-like.

Ears: Very small and alert.

Neck: The neck should be strong, but not too heavy, and neither long nor short— stallions should have a modest crest.

Back: The back, loins and hind-quarters should be strong and well covered with muscle. Tail set high and full.

Feet: Tough and well-shaped.

Action: The action should be low and free, with a typical hack or riding action.

Exmoor

The Exmoor pony—similar in many ways to its neighbour the Dartmoor pony—is an interesting example of how sparse and poor feeding conditions will dwarf a breed. The main growth on the moor is heather and a poor sort of grass—from the top of the many beacons (hills) this type of herbage stretches as far as the eye can see.

In past ages wolves roamed the moor, and the ponies were an easy prey; gradually they were provided by nature with a coat which blended in with the background, one of the many examples of natural camouflage.

During the two World Wars the Exmoor ponies became unpopular with local farmers (who were anxious to raise as many sheep and cattle as possible) as they consumed much of the herbage. They were killed off in large numbers and sold for meat. This, quite naturally, had an adverse effect on the breed and it took some time after the Second War to build it up again.

In the hunting field on the moors, it is quite common nowadays to see strong little Exmoor ponies, ridden by children or even adults, for whilst making ideal children's mounts, they have great endurance and can carry weight.

One feature which is different from all the other native breeds is the texture of the coat, which in winter is harsh and springy and has no sheen on it; in summer it becomes close and hard and produces a shine like brass.

Breed Description

Height: At maturity mares must not exceed 12·2 h.h. and stallions 12·3 h.h.

Colour: Dun or brown, but no white markings or white hairs are permitted anywhere.

Head: The forehead should be wide with prominent eyes (referred to in the breed as frog or toad eyes) the lids of which are slightly hooded like a hawk. The ears are short, thick, pointed and set on a wide forehead, and are a mealy colour on the inside, similar to the colour of the muzzle. The nostrils are wide and of generous proportions.

Body:	The body should have a deep, wide chest with a back of medium length and powerful loins. The shoulders should be set well back.
Legs:	The legs should be clean, with neat hard feet.
General Characteristics:	Inclined to be obstinate, but no more than any other mountain or moorland pony. Excellent as foundation stock that can provide a line of sturdy and intelligent horses. The Exmoor is the oldest British native breed.

Left: portrait of a Champion — an Exmoor pony.

Fell

It is possible to trace the history of this breed back to the times of the Roman occupation of Britain, to the horses of the troops stationed along Hadrian's Wall—the boundary between England and Scotland. A legion called the Cuncus Frisiorium was stationed on the Wall during the last period of the Roman occupation, and they were 'hossed' with Frisian horses from the north of Holland. These Frisian horses are believed by some to be what we now call Fells; indeed Fell owners have even recognised physical characteristics of their own animals in ancient pictures of the Frisians.

Over a hundred years ago a visitor to Cumberland and Westmorland in the north of England would have found it commonplace to see strings of ponies making their way across the narrow paths from the lead mines to the Tyneside and other docks. Each pony would have been carrying sixteen stone (224 pounds) of lead in panniers; with such loads these tough, hardy ponies averaged at least two hundred miles a week and were a vital part of the economic life of the north of England. Most of the Fell ponies used for pannier work came to know the routes they travelled so well that it was often unnecessary to have anyone with them.

In its natural habitat the Fell pony has grown hardy, as the fells and moors are often covered with snow in winter. However, the Fell, like the Dales, has been able to adapt itself to extreme climatic conditions. Numbers of them have been exported to Pakistan, to help breed up pack-ponies for the army from the local mares. The ponies are also used extensively by deer-stalkers, as they are well able to carry the shot stag.

Breed Description

Height: Not over 14 h.h.

Colour: Black, brown, grey and bay, preferably with no white markings, though a star, or a little white on the foot is allowed.

Head: Small, well chiselled in outline, well set on, with a broad forehead, tapering to the nose, with large and expanding nostrils. The eyes should be prominent, bright, mild and intelligent. Ears neatly set on, well formed and small.

Neck: The neck should be of proportionate length, to give a good length of rein, strong and not too heavy, with a moderate crest in the case of the stallion.

Body: A strong back of good outline, with muscular loins, thick through the heart, round-ribbed from shoulders to flank, short and well coupled, hind-quarters square and strong with the tail well set on. The shoulders should be well laid back and sloping, not too fine at the withers.

Legs: The feet should be of good size, round and well-formed. The fore-legs should be straight, well placed and not restricted at the elbows, with big well-formed knees, short cannon bones, with plenty of good flat bone below the knee (at least 8 inches) and with great muscularity of the arm. The hind-legs should have muscular thighs and second thighs, with hocks well let down and clean-cut, with plenty of bone below the joint.

Action: The walk should be smart and true. The trot well-balanced with good knee and hock action, going well from the shoulder and flexing the hocks.

New Forest

A motorist travelling to Southampton, Britain's seaport link with the U.S.A., will drive through the New Forest in Hampshire. It can be a frustrating journey with valuable time lost because of a herd of ponies and their foals idling their time away in the middle of the main road or ambling slowly through a village street. On the other hand, what a wonderful final sight of rural England for the visitor, in this age of rush and bustle. The New Forest is still Crown Property and owners may turn out their ponies to graze there for most of the year and

Left: a Fell pony from the North of England.   **Below:** freedom and space in the New Forest.

to wander where they like.

It was way back in history, almost a thousand years ago, that William the Conqueror afforested this area, calling it the New Forest. The breed of pony found there today is thought to date back to the original ponies which roamed the area in the time of King Canute, a Dane who ruled England even earlier than William . . .

At the end of the 18th Century the Duke of Cumberland, who was appointed to look after the Crown interests in the New Forest, introduced an Arab stallion into the forest to improve the breed, and although after a while the stallion was moved to Yorkshire, he was there long enough to leave his mark. It is claimed that this is the reason for the 'Forester' of today bearing a resemblance to the Arab in the shape of its head.

Whilst having deep bone, this pony is narrower than some of the other breeds, and so has become a popular children's pony. It also has an excellent temperament and doesn't seem to object to children climbing all over it. Foresters are very strong and sure-footed and may be used as family mounts, larger ones being ridden by adults.

A champion New Forest Stallion.

Breed Description

Height: Not exceeding 14·2 h.h.

Colour: Mainly brown or bay, but any colour is accepted other than piebald or skewbald.

Head: Well set on with some characteristics of the Arab, but larger in proportion to the body.

Neck: A little short from throat to chest, but good laid-back shoulders give plenty of length of rein.

Back: Short with strong loins and quarters.

Tail: Well set on, though not too high.

The pony should have a good forearm and second thigh, short cannon bones, good feet, plenty of bone and a good straight action. There are two types of New Forest pony:

(a) Ponies up to 13·2 h.h. lighter in bone than the larger ones, which make ideal hunting ponies for children.

(b) Ponies 13·2 h.h. to 14·2 h.h. with plenty of bone and substance; a strong type able to carry adults.

KEY

Dartmoor		Fell	
Exmoor		Shetland	
New Forest		Highland	
Dales		Connemara	
Welsh			

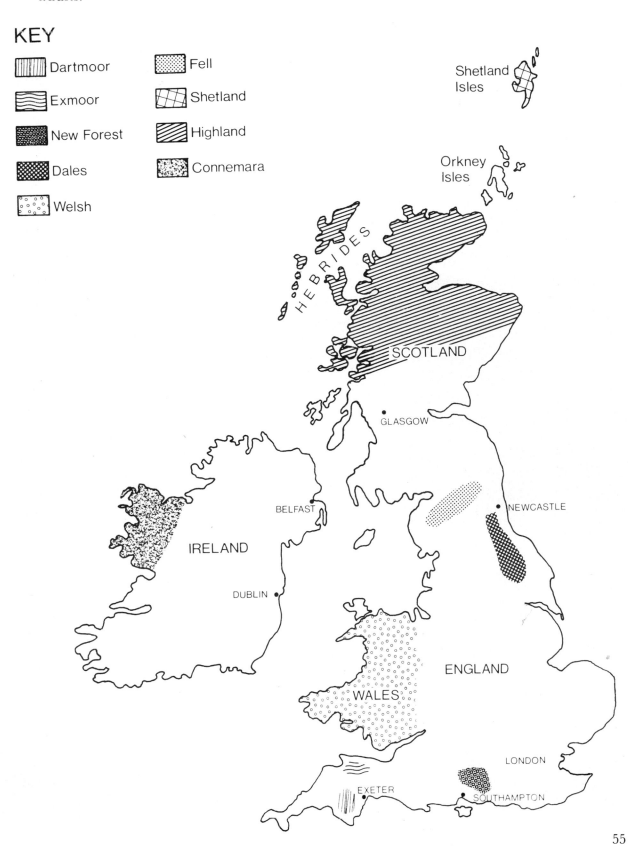

Spotlight on . . . an International Horse Show

The physical beauty of an animal is often at its height when it is active. Muscular exertion, rapid movement, the momentary flight of a horse clearing a big fence, the precision of horse-and-rider in a dressage competition, the clean, lively action of a pony as he trots around the ring . . . these are times when form and movement often blend into fleeting moments of breathtaking beauty, and we see the horse as truly the most noble of all the world's four-footed animals. It is this beauty that inspired some of the most evocative lines written on the horse. They are by farmer-poet Ronald Duncan:

Where in this wide world can man find nobility without pride, friendship without envy, or beauty without vanity? Here; where grace is laced with muscle, and strength by gentleness confined.
He serves without servility; he has fought without enmity. There is nothing so powerful, nothing less violent; there is nothing so quick, nothing more patient.
England's past has been born on his back. All our history is his industry. We are his heirs; he our inheritance.

The Horse.

Here, in the following pages, we take a glimpse of the horse in motion at an international show, one of the most famous that takes place annually in Britain.

Truly international horsemen come from all over Europe to compete in the show jumping classes, and there is more to the show than jumping . . . the dressage brings the best riders in the world into the spot-lit arena, the National Pony Club Mounted Games keep young spectators on the edge of their seats, the military bands keep the air full of music, skilled riders and horses, from the Spanish Riding School of Vienna or the French Cavalry, entertain in a riot of colour and dexterity. For a full week this show of 1,000 horses draws in 10,000 fans a night; in the tiered darkness of the seats they cheer or hold their breath for three hours while the world's finest horses and riders parade before them . . .

Left: showmanship . . . a French huntsman sounds a call to his hounds. **Above:** a familiar sight in the winner's lists, Britain's Harvey Smith, and **right,** fiesta-time at an international show, when a team of Spanish 'Sherry' horses puts on an elegant traditional display.

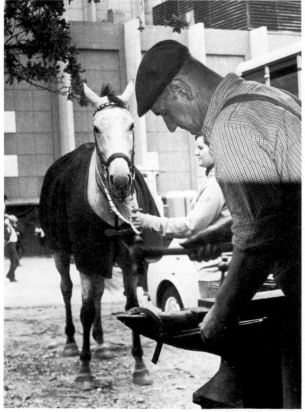

Showtime in the horse world, when the colour and
movement and excitement keeps everyone on their
feet as the tension builds up. The mounting thrill
of the jumping competition is punctuated by displays

of working horses, by gymkhanas, parades,
ponies, the many different breeds on show.
The rider putting her horse over a jump
is one you may recognise —
HRH Princess Anne.

Far left is the world-famous arena at London's Empire Pool (covered over for the occasion) at Wembley. The area is quite small for jumpers, and consequently more difficult to jump. **Left:** rider's-eye view of the arena as the announcer calls for the next to jump. From the dark collecting ring horse and rider walk into the blazing lights of the arena — and into the view of ten thousand critical spectators . . . **Below:** a fanfare from the Cavalry at the start of the Parade.

Appaloosa—Sacred Horse of the East?

American horse culture spans a period of little more than 400 years, dating from the arrival of the invading Spanish *conquistadores* who landed in the New World in the 16th Century, bringing with them the first horses to tread the American continent since the extinction of the small, primitive, indigenous species thousands of years before.

Within that relatively short space of time, however, a surprising number of specifically American breeds have been developed from importations that began with the Spanish invaders and continued up to the arrival of the English thoroughbred almost two centuries later. As a result, America can now claim a place as one of the World's principal horse-breeding countries, boasting, amongst others, such names as the Quarter Horse, the Morgan, the Standard-bred and the Appaloosa.

The evolution of every one of the American breeds makes a fascinating story but none is so colourful, romantic and at times tragic, as the history of the Appaloosa.

The name Appaloosa is no more than 100 years old and the breed can only be said to have received recognition with the formation of the Appaloosa Horse Club as recently as 1937. But, under different names, a breed of spotted horses has existed in Asia and Europe for some 20,000 years certainly, and possibly, in the opinion of some historians, for 30,000 years before that.

An Appaloosa in fine Worcester porcelain . . . and **opposite,** the real thing with rider in smoked buckskin, strings of beads and feathered head-dress of the young American Indian girl of 1870.

Spotted horses, in all shapes and sizes, still occur in many parts of the world outside America, of course; but the point to be made is that all spotted horses are not Appaloosa (indeed, not *all* Appaloosas are spotted). The word Appaloosa refers only to the American counterpart, descended in the main from the herds of the Nez Percé Indians who occupied the Palouse country of Idaho—and particularly the Grande Ronde Valley—from before the coming of the white settler until their virtual extinction in 1877. It is to this tribe and their comparatively advanced practise of selective horse-breeding that the inherent characteristics of the present-day Appaloosa are due.

Cave Drawings

The first evidence of spotted horses, remarkably similar in type to the Appaloosa, is to be seen in the 20,000 year-old cave drawings made by the primitives of Central Europe. These pictures, painted as part of a mystic ritual and used as a means of creating potent magic, may be seen today in the caves at Lascaux and Perche-Merle in France.

Much later in the human progression evidence of the spotted horse, and of the esteem in which he was clearly held, appears in Egyptian pictures of around 1400 BC whilst Asia, especially in the forms of Chinese arts, provides a particularly fertile ground for research; the spotted horse appearing on statues, vases and wall-hangings which can be dated to many hundreds of years earlier.

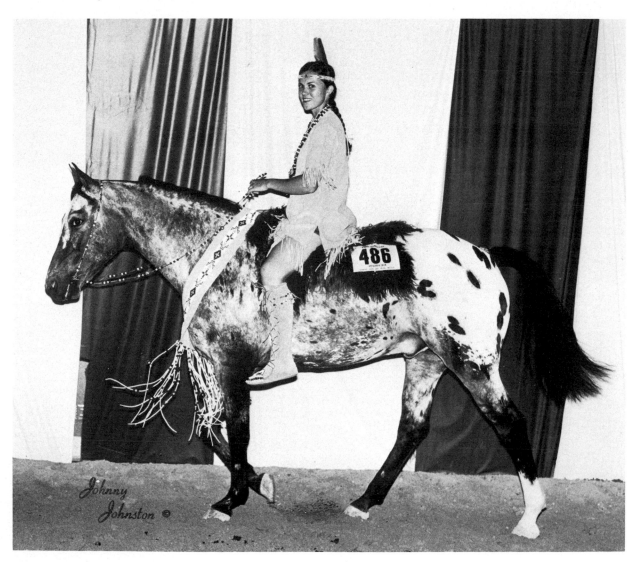

A beautiful Welsh Mountain Pony in Palamino colours.

The Chinese undoubtedly obtained their spotted horses, known variously as the 'Heavenly Horses', the 'Blood-Sweating Breed' or the 'Sacred Horses', from the Persians, the greatest horse breeders of ancient times. The Emperor Wu Ti, for instance, went to war for a quarter of a century in order to obtain a herd of these infinitely superior horses. It was, indeed, fairly common for the Emperors of ancient China to be buried with statuettes of the Sacred Horses to accompany them to their ancestors; or to be speeded on their celestial way by a sacrificial killing of their most beautiful horses.

Persian legend has it that the breed of spotted horses descends from the horse *Rakush*, selected as his mount by the hero *Rustom*. Rustom lived, presumably, around 400 BC and his story and that of Rakush is immortalised in the epic poem *Shah Namah*, written by Firdausi about a thousand years ago.

The spotted horse grew so precious that at night
They burned wild rue to right and left of him
for fear of harm . . .

That of course is legend, but the existence of spotted horses in the far mists of antiquity is fact, and that the Persians developed a particularly fine breed of horses is also amply substantiated.

Closer to our own times the paintings of 17th and 18th Century Europe depict the spotted horse as the mount of kings and nobles, most of them performing the classical airs of what we call the *haute école*. Many of the early horses used at the famous Spanish Riding School are shown, in pictures still in the Riding Hall at Vienna, as being spotted.

These horses were of Spanish or Andalusian ancestry and it is probable that it was from this source that the American Appaloosa derived, being brought over the seas a century or so before by the Conquistadores.

By 1730 horses descended from those originally brought by the Spaniards had spread throughout America, transforming the life of the American Indian by providing him with a new, and until that time, unknown mobility.

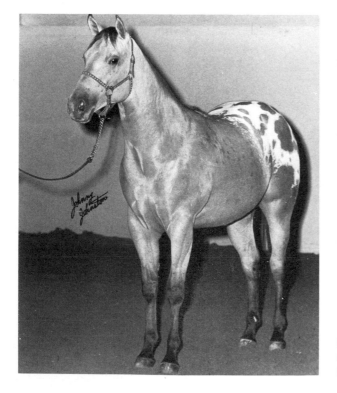

Spots are often more numerous on the quarters, although not all Appaloosas are spotted — and not all spotted horses are Appaloosas.

Horses of the Palouse

It was about this date that spotted horses became apparent in the area of the Palouse River, in the traditional territory of the Nez Percé Indians. The Nez Percé, living in the sheltered, fertile valley of the Grande Ronde, collected great herds of these horses and bred selectively, selling off the poorer stock to their neighbours and gelding colts that did not match up to exacting standards. As stockbreeders the Nez Percé were undoubtedly ahead of their time; as horsemen they must rank with the Mongols of Genghis Khan.

By 1870, when the white man had established himself, settlers had penetrated into Nez Percé country and began to call the horses they saw there Palouse, after the river; then the word became Palousey. It is easy to see how in time 'a Palousey' became 'Appaloosey' and finally Appaloosa.

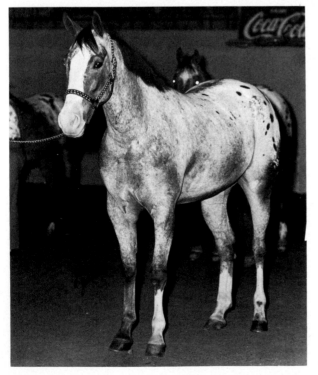

Above: Nez Percé Indians with their horses and, **left,** Red Man's Bluff, a champion Appaloosa.

The distinctive markings of the Appaloosa appealed to the Nez Percé, a people much given to the decorative arts. Other tribes, not possessing horses of this singular coat pattern, frequently painted their war ponies, embellishing them with spots, circles and hand-prints on the rump, such as are occasionally seen on an Appaloosa coat.

Nevertheless, although the colouring of the horses added much to their desirability, the Nez Percé were even more concerned with the practical aspects of the horses they bred so carefully. The Nez Percé required a horse of stamina and speed for hunting and war, and one, also, that was sure-footed enough to cope with the rugged terrain. Additionally, their horses had to have courage combined with an equable temperament if they were to face the bear, buffalo and elk that provided their masters with food and materials, and if they were to carry the braves into battle when the war-drums rolled. Since the land was unfenced the horses roamed free, or largely so, and it was necessary to have a horse 'biddable' enough to come up at the call or whistle of his master.

The End of a Nation

These were the qualities the Nez Percé looked for in their horses and which, though the purposes to which the breed is put are now so different, contribute to the value of the present day Appaloosa as an all-round pleasure horse.

American internal policy, by 1877, was firmly committed to the path of placing the Indian in selected reservations, and its implementation was often harsh and devoid of humanity. The independent Nez Percé, naturally enough, resisted attempts to make them give up the land which their forefathers had regarded as theirs for generations. So they fought, with bow, arrow, spear and out-of-date rifle from the backs of their spotted horses, against the might of troops equipped with artillery and modern firearms and supported by the whole paraphenalia of European-type warfare. Most of the time, refusing the conventional text-book battle, they emerged as victors and in the process occasionally made the United States Army look somewhat foolish.

Inevitably, however, the continuing battle of attrition could have but one end. With the warriors of the tribe decimated, and faced with a continually reinforced enemy, the chief of the Nez Percé, Chief Joseph, embarked on a fighting retreat aimed at taking what remained of the tribe to the comparative safety of Canada. He would have succeeded had he not, having reached the Missouri, mistakenly thought that he had crossed the border. The Nez Percé had fought and marched the 1800 miles up to the Bear Paw Mountains in Montana, engaging the troops on eleven occasions, five of which might be considered as major battles. Appreciating, too late, his error, Chief Joseph made his last stand at the Missouri with just 87 warriors, 40 of whom were wounded. In the light snow that fell on that early October day in 1877 the final chapter was written in the history of the Nez Percé nation. Previously they had repulsed Colonel Miles' frontal charge with 600 troopers but in the end there was nothing left but to surrender. It was made with dignity by Chief Joseph in the famous speech ending 'Now hear me, oh my chiefs. I am tired. My heart is sick and sad. From where the sun now stands, I will fight no more for ever.'

He and the gallant remnants of his tribe should have received the consideration due to brave and skilful opponents, but there was no magnanimity in victory accorded by the conquering forces of civilisation. The tribe's wealth, its means of existence and its hope of regeneration—the 'Palouse' horses—were slaughtered, or at least those within reach of the troopers' rifles.

And there, to all intent, the nation of the Nez Percé ceased to exist. But in a way, the name of the Nez Percé was to live on through their horses, although they, too, were to come near to extinction.

Indeed it was not until 1937, when only a few hundred of the pure breed remained, that public interest was aroused. In that year, through the agency of Claude Thompson, the Appaloosa Horse Club was formed. By its efforts the Appaloosa is now widely bred and even more widely appreciated, and the Club has become one of the largest in America.

The hereditary toughness and versatility of the Appaloosa and his excellent temperament suit him for almost every form of horse sport. He is used as a cow-pony, a pleasure horse, for trail-riding, polo and show-jumping and appears to excel at them all. In this last sport Appaloosas are now said to be frequently jumping seven feet, and it is a thoroughbred Appaloosa cross that holds the world record for the half-mile.

The colouring is, of course, a notable characteristic of the Appaloosa and is quite distinctive whatever the pattern. Nostrils and lips are invariably part-coloured and the sclera of the eye is white. The forepart of the body is either of one colour or of a mottled roan, whilst the loins and hind-parts are lighter coloured, or white, with dark, round or egg-shaped spots which stand up from the rest of the coat. Some Appaloosas are white with what are known as 'leopard' spot markings covering the whole body. The feet are equally distinctive, usually displaying vertical black and white stripes whilst the horn is particularly dense.

The tail of the Appaloosa may often be wispy and almost rat-like, a practical sort of appendage for a horse reared for use in thick scrub country well supplied with thorn.

The Appaloosa is not a big horse—14·2–15 h.h. is the average height—but he is compact, showing great strength in the quarters, and standing on short legs. In fact, he is expected to have the balance and attributes of a good riding horse, and in its judging guide the Appaloosa Horse Club emphasises this requirement by allotting 40 per cent for conformation, the remaining 60 per cent being equally divided between type, soundness and action.

The Appaloosa was accepted as a breed by the National Association of Stallion Registration Boards in 1950. Perhaps, on that day, the spirits of the warriors who fell at the Missouri and on the long trail from the Grande Ronde Valley rested easy at last in the happy hunting grounds.

These lovely young Lipizzaners at Piber in Austria
are destined for the Spanish Riding School of Vienna.

Straight from the Horse's Mouth

A horse's mouth is more often than not a most neglected part of his body. Yet it can tell us so much, that *ideally, we should look in our horse's mouth as often as we pick out his feet.* If we did we would sometimes be stricken with remorse, particularly after a day's hunting, when it is just possible that we should see the effects of too-heavy hands on the sensitive bars and unprotected corners of the lips.

Then there is the young horse who, up to the age of six (when he is said to have a 'full mouth'), is constantly shedding milk teeth and replacing them with permanent ones. Very often these youngsters will quite suddenly become fractious about the head, throwing it about and evading all the signals given by our hands. Some silly folk (not like you and me of course) then rush to the saddler's shop to buy a new bit which they think might solve the problem.

Wise folk look in the horse's mouth. Nine times out of ten the poor animal is teething, and his gums will be found to be inflamed. No wonder that in this condition he becomes irritable —just like a human baby in a similar situation. A few day's rest and all will be well; we shall have saved the price of a new bit and, most probably, we shall have prevented a temporary resistance from becoming an ingrained habit.

Older horses, too, can experience trouble with their teeth and will react in the same way. In their case, however, it may be caused by a split or diseased tooth, one which you wouldn't know about unless you took a look; or it could be a 'wolf' tooth, or perhaps the teeth have worn sharp and are causing discomfort.

Wolf teeth appear in front of the molars, the grinding teeth at the back; they cause pain whilst erupting through the gum and once *in situ* interfere with the placing of the bit. The remedy is to have them removed.

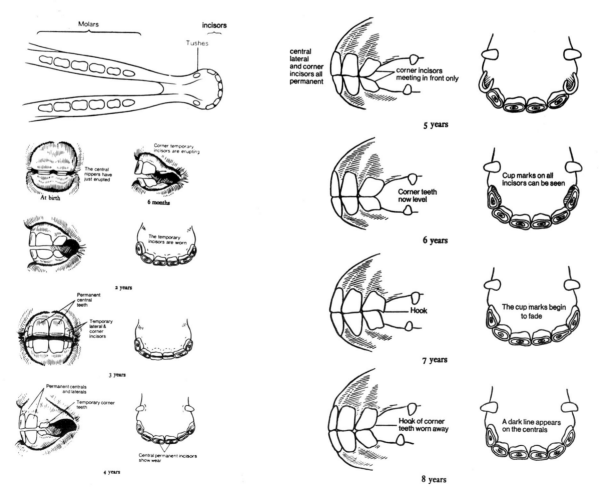

The molars, too, can wear sharp. A horse's upper jaw is wider than the lower, and the molars on the former grow downwards and outwards whilst the corresponding teeth on the lower jaw grow upwards and inwards. Consequently the top molars receive little wear on the outer edge and the lower ones little wear on the inner edge. Both can become as sharp as a razor and then our poor horse may lacerate his cheeks and even his tongue. Teeth edges should be filed by a veterinarian before they cause that particular trouble.

Open, Please!

Of course, one has first to open the mouth before its mysteries can be revealed, and this is something that so many people find difficult and so many horses find uncomfortable. In reality opening a mouth is simplicity itself if you are gentle and use a little commonsense. Stand alongside the horse, just in front of his shoulder and then, using a hand on either lip part them gently, taking care that the topmost hand does not cover the horse's nostrils and impede breathing.

To open the mouth insert your thumb and forefinger, held on either side, onto the bars of the lower jaw (i.e. the fleshy gum area between the molar and incisor teeth). If you do this quietly, keeping the other hand resting lightly on the nose well above his nostrils, he will open up most obligingly.

The teeth fulfill other functions in addition to chewing up food or taking a piece out of your breeches. They are the only way open to us of estimating the horse's age. Even experienced horsemen, however, can make mistakes in this respect and, after a horse has reached ten years, not even the most experienced can calculate age with absolute accuracy. However, until all horses are branded with their date of birth (which would be the most convenient solution for most of us, if one not entirely welcome to some horse-dealers) examination of the teeth provides the only evidence of age.

Each jaw of the horse contains 12 molar teeth and six incisors, the biting teeth. Male horses also grow 'tushes', tusk-like teeth, behind the incisors, for reasons which have yet to be satis-

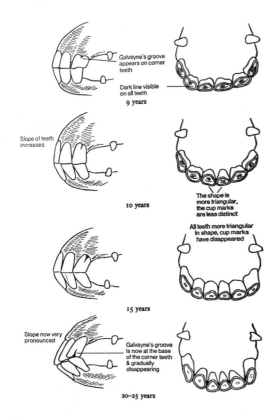

Galvayne's groove appears on corner teeth

Dark line visible on all teeth
9 years

Slope of teeth increases

10 years

The shape is more triangular, the cup marks are less distinct

All teeth more triangular in shape, cup marks have disappeared

15 years

Slope now very pronounced

Galvayne's groove is now at the base of the corner teeth & gradually disappearing

20–25 years

factorily explained. It is by examining the shape, size and markings of the incisor teeth that we can estimate the horse's age.

The Foal's Teeth

Newly-born foals have no teeth, although you may be able to see the central incisors through the gum. After ten days these are cut and within four to six weeks are followed by the lateral incisors. At between six and nine months a foal cuts his corner incisors and then has a full set of milk teeth. These milk teeth are easily recognisable by their colour, which is white rather than the yellow of permanent teeth, and they all taper to a definite point at the base. The horse does not start to lose his milk teeth until he is a three-year-old.

Two and Three Years Old

The horse still has milk teeth at two but now 'marks' or cups will be seen on the tables.

At three years the horse will have replaced the two central milk teeth with permanent incisors, but will retain two milk teeth on either side of them.

Four Years Old

The lateral incisors are now replaced by permanent teeth, leaving only two milk teeth, the corner incisors, in each jaw. The central incisors now show cups on the tables; the two new laterals are unmarked. In the male horse the tushes, behind the incisors, will now have broken through the gum. Very ocasionally mares will grow tushes, but it is unusual.

Five Years Old

The last of the milk teeth, the corner ones, are now replaced by permanent incisors, and except for these new arrivals all the teeth have cups on the tables. Because these new teeth have received no wear, the upper and lower ones will only meet at the front edge. The horse now has a full mouth of permanent teeth.

Six Years Old

From now on the accurate assessment of age is more difficult and factors of wear and changing shapes must be considered. At six, however, the corner teeth provide a useful guide. These will have now worn level and will meet along the whole surface. All teeth have clear cup markings and in the male the tush is fully grown.

Seven Years Old

Most noticeable at this age is the change in the cups on all the teeth. They are now less distinct, and the outlines have lost their former sharpness. Once again the corner incisor is helpful. At seven it has developed into a hook shape which overlaps the rear of its partner.

Eight Years Old

The hook on the corner incisor has now worn away. The cups on all teeth are very indistinct, particularly on the central incisors. In addition a new mark, a dark line at the forward edge of the tables of these teeth, is quite noticeable. This is called *Galvayne's groove*.

From Nine Upwards

Galvayne's groove at nine is $\frac{1}{4}$ inch long and a change is noticeable in the size and shape of the teeth. They are now longer, project to the front and are becoming triangular in shape.

The diagrams show the changes which take place from ten onwards fairly clearly, but it should be remembered that the teeth take on a more pronounced slope as the years go by; they are longer, no cups are visible at all on the tables, and each tooth becomes more triangular in shape. Galvayne's groove will be halfway down the corner incisor at 15 years and reaches the bottom of the tooth at 20 years.

An Englishwoman in America

Jennifer Stobart comes from England, and has spent most of the last ten years in Canada and the United States, as a riding instructress. Here she tells us of some of her life in North America...

I never dreamt that life with horses would give me such wonderful entertainment, travel and a chance to meet so many interesting people. I suppose I expected to settle in some peaceful English stable-yard with a day's hunting or a horse show providing the main excitement; but all that changed when I decided to try my luck in the United States of America. There is much more Trans-Atlantic communication now in the horse world than there was ten years ago, perhaps due to some private visits and individuals showing on both sides, but more still to the chance people have had to see the U.S. jumping team in action in Europe, and various Pony Club exchanges in both directions.

When I landed in Canada I knew virtually nothing about the different 'way of going' and I was so lucky to start in a place where there were English style hacks, American style hunters, equitation classes for juniors and one day events, dressage competitions, hunter pace events and open jumping, gaited and Western horses!

My introduction to some of these came at the large Fall Show and Rodeo at Calgary, where we (my girl companion and I) stopped to stay with family friends on the way West. We went night after night, fascinated by every class, especially by the Saddle bronc riding and the Bramha bulls! My most vivid memory, however is of the stunned amazement we felt when the Arab Mounted Costume class came into the arena. We'd been aware of shadows milling around out in the darkness of the holding ring, and then the gates were flung open and into the ring rushed a swirl of dazzling, glittering colours—yelling, galloping—how marvellous, and how very un-English! I never did quite discover how the class is judged because the horses are so covered up with draperies that you can only see their knees and noses! Little did I think then that I'd be taking part in such a class myself the next summer, at the Pacific National Exposition, plus beard to add to my costume!

It started for me in a little town called Haney, in British Columbia, about 30 miles from Vancouver, where there was a large riding centre. I went there by invitation to teach, ride and train.

It is fall when I arrive—golden cottonwoods and crisp mornings with snow on the mountain tops. There are young horses to train, and the cream of the area's horses are off with their junior riders to the Toronto Royal Winter Fair. When they get back, weary from the long rail trip but with their fair share of ribbons, we turn them out to play. They nearly turn themselves inside out with the joy of being free again, rolling, squeaking and exploding—sending up clouds of snow in all directions.

When January came I learned something about why there were so many Dutch people in the area. Their knowledge of dykes and flood control was vital to prevent what nearly happened—in the flat valley land the water level had been rising fast and banks were on the point of over-flowing and breaking. There was a dramatic afternoon in torrential rain when horses had to be evacuated to higher land across a flooded bridge. Have you ever tried to ride, lead, drive and swim reluctant Arabs through icy water? It's not their best 'thing'!

Victoria Show

I remember crossing from the mainland to Vancouver Island on a lovely sunny day, en route for the Victoria Show with a truckload of horses. We were escorted by seagulls as we steamed past little islands, having left from the most suitable-sounding Horseshoe Bay, and as we looked back we could see the unforgettable background of mountains of the Cascade Range.

I was worried about what sort of fences I would find, and how the young horses would behave. For them and me it was our first 'recognised' show away from the Centre, and there were many rumours about a fearful Liverpool built for the open jumpers. But the horses went well, and it was impressive to be receiving ribbons from the Governor of the province.

By now I had learnt something of the American style of showing hunters. I'd never taken it terribly seriously before if my horse played up a bit in a hunter class under saddle; now I had to concentrate on never breaking pace, which I found very quenching. I *still* feel that it spoils a lot of the enjoyment in having a horse moving well, since you have to be so careful

Left: Riding hall and stabling at Foxcroft School in Virginia. **Above:** Jennifer Stobart at a British Pony Club Camp.

73

Judging the Arab Costume Class . . .

while trying to look so relaxed, and sometimes the way out best horse makes a little mistake and loses the class, for no great fault. To my mind, the most effective part of the American system is the smooth pace required over fences. It was a new experience to me to watch horses go round a course at such an even pace, meeting their fences right in stride. It looks very polished and relaxed and isn't always so easy to achieve! One thing no one thought to tell me was what eliminated you on an outside course—until a young horse failed to rise at a fence with me and we both tipped over in the mud. I was quite surprised to find I wasn't expected to finish the course! As for the junior equitation classes, I thought they were out-standingly successful, and had to be a tremendous training ground for every young rider.

The whole summer seemed to whizz by; classes to teach, shows to plan for, organise and travel to—and recover from. The Pacific National was the longest—it seemed to last for weeks. Sometimes I'd go home in the early hours of the morning after a delicious midnight meal of barbecued chicken or smoked salmon from the nearby booths (for who could eat before jumping in the evening classes?); then back next day to braid and start again, after maybe teaching a morning class at the Centre, bringing with me a sack of freshly picked grass for those fussy feeders who were sick of living indoors, and whose appetites had to be titivated. I had to take particular care to keep Bonaparte, my open jumper, eating. He was a very high-strung type, tho' most dependable in the ring, and we'd been having a very good summer together. We'd been second so many times; jumping off against the clock he would try so hard to go clear but hadn't got the speed of some of his thoroughbred rivals. He was good in the

Puissance classes, and won the 6-Bar at the P.N.E., much to my delight, as I'd always thought that was a most exciting type of competition and a good test of suppleness and impulsion. His consistency paid off, anyway, for at the end of the year he was High Score Jumper for his Zone.

There were five of us girls, four English and one Dutch, working at or near the Centre, and I don't think we took many days off during the busy season, but we'd had good days of skiing on the local mountains, and made a few trips across the border down to Mount Baker for bigger slopes. I had my worst wreck down there, falling off the top of a ski lift, in helpless laughter, because I was waiting for it to stop for me to dismount!

Dressage in New York State

Soon after that, new opportunities led me back East to cross the border and settle for a while in New York State. There I spent some months, mainly indoors, because it was winter again, in the dedicated atmosphere of advanced dressage. There were stallions to ride, thoroughbred and Lipizzaner, Pony Club horses to train, and lessons to give to clients who were so keen that they would even make an eight o'clock a.m. class, coming more than 40 miles from New York City! Some weekends there would be six or seven instructors teaching at the same time in three languages—luckily all our voices and accents were easily distinguishable, but the clients surely had to concentrate!

Above: Eastern Dressage Championships at Hideaway Farm, Genesco, New York, in August 1971; Miss Kie Johnson on Fleury. **Left:** Jennifer Stobart riding Bonaparte at Vancouver, B.C.

That summer I found myself in Iowa—and, less than a month later, committed to ride a strange horse that I had only sat on once in a National Three Day Event in California. Luckily he was a very good performer, and I had lots of confidence in his owner. We were to share the driving out to Pebble Beach, and the plan was to take five horses in all, one behind our wagon, and four more to come separately in a cattle truck. The corn belt was straight out of 'Oklahoma' —the corn *was* as high as an elephant's eye. We were each riding nearly six hours a day on various horses to get ourselves fit, and we must have set up a world record for the quantity of iced tea we got through. The drive through Kansas (surely an extra wide state), a corner of Texas, New Mexico and Arizona was another new experience—I was used to long distances between gas stations by then, but to see 'last chance for ICE for 80 miles' really made me think!

It didn't take us very long to recover—we had a weekend of Dressage Championships before the Three Day started, which served to acclimatise us nicely. The arena there was so attractively set in amongst the pine trees, and the footing was perfect. The only formidable aspect was the panel of most distinguished international judges. The biggest surprise for our Iowa bred horses was the SEA—they couldn't believe it was really true, and as for the seals . . . my 'Copper Horn' produced a classic *passage* along the shore when they started to bark! That was a beautiful course to ride, well marked, and the fences were very fair. The only serious worry for us was during the steeplechase phase which was laid out on one of the famous golf courses. We were all warned that anyone straying onto a fairway would be eliminated on the spot, which made it a little hard to concentrate on the inviting aiken fences . . .

I went back to California ten years later, to lecture and judge at a combined training event, this time inland near Sacramento. A great course had been built. Eucalyptus groves, natural drops, white board paddock fences and even the hop farm elevators had been used to produce a very good test.

At School in Virginia

How to describe the years in between? I spent them mainly in Virginia, with many side trips to other states for various sessions; judging, competing, teaching. My job was at a girls' boarding school—one of those special ones where your horse can come along too. And the horses did, from all over! The big vans would roll in, in September, from Florida or Texas, Maryland or Minnesota, New Jersey or Kentucky, usually in the middle of the night, it seemed. Trunks, record players and bicycles travelled to and from home this way too—much more safely than by regular freight routes.

We tried to offer a varied riding programme—I think similar schools in nearby states were working along the same lines, but none could have had better facilities than we acquired through the tremendous generosity of one parent, who donated a new yard of 60 fine stalls, with barns, tack rooms, offices, and a vast indoor ring. The land had always been there—the best possible for riding; hilly, wooded in part, Goose Creek winding through it all and the Blue Ridge mountains behind.

The seasons gave a natural variety to our activities, and with the indoor hall to count on these were never grounded. Fall was for larking on cross-country hacks, cubbing with its early starts on dark Saturday mornings, race meetings at Glenwood, then hunting proper—a cow horn sounding mournfully in the woods, stone walls, coops, and splashy crossings at Goose Creek's fords. I was never supposed to look back and count 'my' girls—by the time they were competent to hunt they *were* competent, but I did enjoy watching them sometimes over fences! The Inter-School-and-College Horse Trials were usually fitted into that term and a select few would take off for the Washington International Show and 'The Garden'.

We were very lucky in the gift horses that kind people would donate to the school. They were a tremendous help in mounting good riders who did not have a horse of their own at school, and some turned into ideal teaching types. I adopted one charming thoroughbred mare, Sugar Foot, who turned out to be rather too strong for most juniors, and I had a great time working with her. She competed in a few One Day Events, but then we discovered that she had become blind in one eye, and this upset her focusing, so her jumping became rather wild. She moved so nicely and had such lovely rhythm that I continued with her dressage training, and took her up to 4th Level, which meant that she was doing lateral work, shoulder-in and half-pass, really good extended trots, and flying changes. I used to take her around to any competitions within reach, and one of her greatest successes was in winning a qualifying class for the A.H.S.A. Senior Class finals.

Left: 'Spots', mascot for one of the Foxcroft basketball teams.

Hunter Trials, with a Californian beach in the background.

Hunting—and the School Show

Christmas vacations gave me the chance to fit in some marvellous hunting trips to other packs. Georgia produced grand runs with the Midland Foxhounds; their vines down there are *tough*, and I learnt to leave my whip at home after the first day, so that I'd have a spare hand to untangle myself when necessary. We had a new sort of storm—to me—while I was there; in fact it held me up and I was nearly late getting back to school—an ice storm enclosed all the highways, and left the pecan trees looking like something out of a fairy-tale, all sheathed in icicles.

Once I went out to Colorado in December. I'd been to Denver during the summer to teach Pony Clubs and I was invited back to enjoy several days with the Arapahoe Hunt. I was lent a super horse who knew all about what was going on. This time the snow was down, several inches of it, covering all the gopher holes and hazards and rounding off the ridges. I don't believe that I've ever before had such a glorious, timeless feeling of galloping almost endlessly over those great snowy Sections, with the dark blob of a coyote coasting easily ahead of the racing hounds.

Winter term was something of an endurance test. Thick warm clothes didn't make for supple riders on cold horses, and snow sliding off the roof could create instant impulsion! When you went outside, too, certain horses loved to drop down with absolutely no warning into a snow drift to roll, but it was a soft landing, anyway!

Spring term always flew by. The highlight was the school Horse Show in early May, which was open to the public, and to any of our sister schools who could send a team of riders. The

A reminder of the Motherland . . . a private coach
leaves Windsor for the racing at Ascot.

preparations were immense, and all the judges donated their efforts, as the profits went to local charities. The equitation classes were held ahead of the show day, as every rider in the school had a level in which to compete. The school horses had to work extra hard to make sure that everyone had the best chance of a 'good trip' as possible. It was fun to see everyone turned out smartly, after the every-day wear of jeans and sweaters, and the grounds always looked their best, newly mown, and trimmed with cedars on all the fences. We used to set a course for the top 'hunt girls' that would combine part of a good outside course with a finish over some tight stadium fences, and they were always given a good work-out on the flat first, so they really had a good test.

After the show was over, we could relax a little more for the last few weeks of the school year and enjoy going off cross-country. If it was hot enough we would spend some time paddling or even swimming in Goose Creek, something that the horses enjoyed at least as much as their riders. Some warm days we would get out really early and go off into the mist before breakfast, and vow that this was the very best time of all. I still can't decide which *is* the best season in Virginia—as each one came round it seemed to be the loveliest, and the fall was very hard to beat, with the colours and smells of damp leaves, the stooks of corn and misty bottoms to the valleys. Then would come the stark black and white of empty branches and snow, and the joy of looking back at your hoof-prints to discover that you had ridden in a nearly-perfect circle . . .! And then spring would creep up, with carpets of daffodils and a misty look of dogwood in the woods—it really is too difficult to decide, but I am glad that I have known them all . . .

The weeks I've spent teaching Pony Clubs have taken me to some wonderful places. South Woodstock, Vermont, the home of the Green Mountain Horse Association, always gives me the same feeling as I used to get going to Scotland in August, when my father and brothers would shoot and fish, and my sister and I would explore the hills and heather. The air on the hills above Woodstock smells almost the same, of myrtle and birch maybe, and the views across to the White Mountains are fabulous. Upwards of 100 horses were all stabled at the GMHA grounds in their fine permanent stalls, and the riders were all 'billeted' close by. We'd work towards a final One-Day event, every group taking its turn to practice each phase; dressage and stadium jumping in the surrounding work areas along the valley; cross-country 'up the hill' (and a steep hill it was, too), where there was a tremendous assortment of fences of every height and degree of difficulty. Always, too there were those gorgeous views in the background, if a rider ever had time to look!

Sessions in Colorado were equally picturesque and the flowers there in June or July were quite breathtaking. Indian paintbrush was always one of my favourites, both for the name and its shades of flame colour. One of the highlights for me was being allowed to help move cattle early in the mornings on the ranch where I was staying, before setting off for my Pony Club Groups. It was fascinating to watch the experts at work, having such control without ever seeming to hurry. I felt a bit like an old English sheep-dog!

Ten years after I first landed in Canada I finally managed to make my first trip to the Royal Winter Fair at Toronto. It was everything I'd expected it to be—and more. The showmanship involved in the vast displays and the speed and timing of the classes in the huge main arena were of the highest standard and I could quite see what a tremendous impact it had made on our riders from British Columbia. For myself, I enjoyed seeing the International jumping classes, the coaching classes (which almost made me homesick) and seeing once more the stunning Arab Horse Mounted Costume class. The hunter courses were most solid and realistically rustic and rode beautifully; I longed to hear the impressions of the distinguished Englishman who was judging them. I left the show almost confused as to which country I was in—but found my bearings as soon as I left the arena and saw those striking mounted police wearing dark capes and fur caps, saw the maple leaf flag flapping overhead, and the cold waves breaking quietly along the peaceful lake shore. I remembered then that I was born a quarter Canadian, and was a much at home as I wanted to be.

Ireland's Beautiful Pony

A visitor to the Emerald Isle should not only go to the west coast to see the sun set on Galway Bay, as the song tells us, but also to see the beautiful Connemara pony, with its handsome head and long mane and tail. The Connemara is the only surviving native pony of Ireland, a sad reflection when the whole world looks upon Ireland as being the home of the horse. The reason for this has again been the development of the country by man, in order to produce the maximum yield from the countryside.

The Connemara comes from the west of Ireland and its natural habitat is the area to the west of Loughs Carrib and Mask, bounded on the west by the Atlantic Ocean, and on the south by Galway Bay.

For centuries a native breed of pony ran wild on the mountains. It is said that some four or five hundred years ago certain rich merchants decided to import some of the finest Arab stallions they could find. As the years went by some of these stallions escaped and ran wild on the mountains with the native ponies, producing the forerunner of the Connemara pony as we know it today—unique in the world, with the strength and hardiness of a mountain pony, combined with the beauty and agility of the Arab.

The west coast of Ireland, exposed to the full force of the Atlantic storms and gales, has made the pony very hardy; and the herbage on which it feeds is very poor. Because of these extreme conditions, the native pony remained small, seldom exceeding 13 h.h., although now, given reasonable conditions, the breed has become somewhat larger and the maximum height allowed by its breed society is 14·2 h.h.

The pony has proved popular in America, too, and there is now an American Connemara Society with its headquarters in Massachusetts.

Breed Description

Height: 13 h.h. to 14·2 h.h.
Colour: Grey, black, bay, brown, dun, with occasional roans and chestnuts. The predominant colour is grey, and in fact, of all those registered more than half are grey. Some years ago, Palomino, golden with white mane and tail, was predominant.
Head: Well-balanced head and neck.
Back: The body should be compact and deep, standing on short legs.
Bone: The bone should be clean, hard and flat, approximately 7 to 8 inches below the knee. Plenty of bone is apparent, the quality of which in all probability cannot be beaten by any breed of pony anywhere in the world.

The Connemara pony is intelligent, hardy,
sure-footed, and an ideal mount for children —
who could ask for more?

The Smallest Horse in the World

It seems as though history has taken a backward turn, at least in the equine world. Back into the past, a million years ago, the modern horse Equus, appeared. But long before Equus, in an age called Oligocene, a little herd animal, the ancestor of today's horse, roamed the plains of Europe. The leaves of the trees were his diet, fleetness of foot his protection against predators. He was about 24 inches high—and took about 35 million years to grow into today's elegant horse. It took a South American rancher just a few short years to turn the clock back and produce the world's smallest horse since those pre-historic days.

Señor Julio Fallabella's father first decided to breed a miniature horse from a small racing thoroughbred at his ranch, and since then hundreds of tiny thoroughbreds—with an occasional dash of Shetland to keep the size down—have been foaled on the pampas near the farm.

They are all under 7 hands high—between 25 and 30 inches—and although some of them will wander like pets into the ranch they are, in effect, in a wild state, fending for themselves the year round.

And what a fashionable pet this tiny horse makes—a fact that has been noticed by some South American families, who have bought one from Julio Fallabella. Others have been bought for more commercial reasons, and are used in ore mines in the region.

Some Fallabellas have been broken in to ride (by very small children) and some to drive. They have a friendly temperament, are more intelligent than many breeds, and once they learn to trust their rider, are easy to handle. And, curiously for such small animals, they have a turn of speed that often surprises their young riders.

All between 27 and 30 inches tall, these diminutive Fallabellas are the smallest horses. These belong to one of the two British owners of examples of the breed.

How did these terrier-sized equines get down to that size? There's still some controversy about the subject. Some allege that a herd was confined for generations in a South American canyon and had only cactus to eat, a diet that slowly reduced their height and general conformation.

Señor Fallabella himself states that they are the result of years of experimenting with genes and inbreeding. Some scientists reject this as virtually impossible, arguing that a horse of less than quarter-size could never be bred this way, and that these miniatures must have been bred from a freak dwarf horse, carrying a dwarfing gene. Other learned theorists aver that the Fallabellas are products of mutations obtained through changes in the structure of genes and chromosomes, a process which is apparently fairly common, and that the present generations have been bred down by selecting the characteristics of a miniature. No doubt some luck and much patience has gone into the breeding of this charming little animal during the fifty years the Fallabella family have been interested in it.

There are few Fallabellas outside South America. In Britain only two owners are known, but this number may increase if breeding plans are successful.

Fallabellas could become the family favourites of the near future. With their pleasant characters, and the universal charm of the miniature, their future would seem to be assured—perhaps as alternatives to the aristocratic Russian Borzoi used in front of the cameras as a model-girl accessory. Or maybe it will replace the poodle as the 'town' pet? Or shall we see a children's Derby—mounts to be under seven hands, and jockeys less than four feet tall?

Shy but intelligent, Fallabellas make good mounts for the smallest of children, and have a surprising turn of speed.

Workhorses of the World . . .

Half-past six in the bright morning. The Greek sea is still at this hour and splashes gently on the shore that separates it from the houses. Up on the mountainside a tethered donkey brays at the sound of hooves below him. It is a jogging horse pulling a cart. His tail flicks idly. He wears a blue beaded collar and a brass bell that wakes the villagers. At every house he stops and his driver scrambles down, seizes the dustbin and empties its contents into the cart. This is the *scupithia*, and he treks round and round the village in the morning gathering up the garbage and clomping out to the dump half a mile beyond the last house. He is an ugly, utilitarian horse; no Greek keeps a horse for pleasure. Some years his ribs show, depending on whether the previous winter was good or bad. In his village at the foot of the Pelopponese there is little keep in the summer except hay; only the goats can chew a living from the barren mountainside.

On the island of Spetsos there are no cars. Instead, transport is by horse and carriage, mainly for the benefit of the tourists. The tourist trade—unlike the garbage collecting trade—is a competitive one, and each outfit vies with its neighbour for sleekness and fitness of horse and shininess of the old-fashioned, open carriage. In summer the drivers wait in a row and argue fiercely over the merits of their respective animals while the latter rest on somnolent legs, their beads and bells drooping, taking a little time off from the eternal round of work . . .

The Heavy Horses

Perhaps the best-known of the world's heavy horses are those that were used in the British Isles for work on the farm, and for road haulage, until about 40 years ago. From the days when the knights of the Middle Ages would ride their great Shires into battle, to the present-day when most of the 'heavies' are seen under the arc-lights in the show ring or showing their paces at local agricultural meetings, Britain has been known for its heavy breeds.

Until the early 1930's there were around 700,000 farm horses still in use in England and Wales, until their sharp decline with the second World War and the arrival of farm mechanisation.

For a while it seemed that they must die out altogether, but as recently as five years ago some farmers realised that the heavy horse still has his uses, and indeed some advantages over the tractor. He can work on heavy or steep terrain where a tractor would be dangerous, he is more economical than a machine, and, for some farm hands, the more extensive care he requires is an infinitely more rewarding task than that of looking after an indifferent tractor.

Shires, Suffolk Punches, Clydesdales and cross-breds are seen once more at work in the countryside or clumping proudly round the show-ring in their finery. Heavy horses are still used extensively on the European Continent and they are also becoming popular in the United States, where they are used in shows and for pleasure driving.

Once they were part of the everyday scene; now working horses are a rarity in the fields. However, some still pull a plough on difficult land, others draw brewers' drays through the twisting roads of old English towns . . . but most are members of the leisured classes . . .

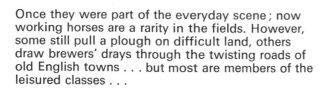

In Great Britain, the heavy horse is by no means limited to the plough; they are also employed by some breweries. Whitbread's Brewery have kept a stable of Shire Horses in the City of London for many years and on short hauls it is actually cheaper to deliver the barrels by horse rather than by truck. Each year since 1954 six of these 'City' Shires, all greys, have donned their ornamental trappings and been harnessed to the magnificent Lord Mayor's Coach to take their place in the Lord Mayor's Show.

Stock Horses

The Camargue, where the mistral howls and the black fighting bulls roam the marshes, has been described as the Wild West of France. These bulls are herded by the *guardiens* on their tough, spirited little grey horses whose fine-boned structures show evidence of the ancient Barb lineage. These horses keep going effortlessly all day over the soggy ground; with their powers of instant acceleration they are ideal for working with the wily bulls, and the guardiens, who spend long hours in the saddle, appreciate their easy, comfortable stride.

In Canada and the States, the Quarter Horse is becoming increasingly popular as a stock horse. Quick and versatile, he has an instinctive knowledge of cattle, and a highly trained cutting horse will work virtually on his own.

Quarter Horse cross-breds and those of less recognisable descent are also used at dude ranches and large tourist hotels such as those in the Rocky Mountains. Here the horses are kept in pony barns; the cowboys in charge have a thorough knowledge of their individual characters and will allocate them to suitable riders accordingly. Even so, it is hard to judge before hand the compatability of horse and rider; many a tourist who said carelessly that of course he's ridden all his life has ended up wrapped round a tree through lack of steering ability!

Shire, Percheron, Clydesdale, Suffolk Punch —
they were the breeds that once kept England's
country tilled and England's people fed. Now they
are seen in a different role — at agricultural and
horse shows throughout the country, parading in
their majestic finery for our pleasure.

The horses go out on three or four rides a day, meandering along the mountain paths or cantering dustily on the lower tracks. In the evening they are herded down to the deep parts of the forest where there is water and lush grass and where they mingle with the mule deer and elk for an hour or so to roll, scratch and graze contentedly. Those in charge chew tobacco, or smoke, resting easily on their mounts but keeping a vigilant eye on would-be strayers, who wear a clanking bell round their necks. At dusk they gather the herd together and head back up the trail; the horses jostle each other excitedly and accelerate at the thought of their oats waiting in the barn, and the journey home becomes a sneezing, dusty gallop punctuated by the din of bells and encouraging cries of the cowboys.

Barby is a typical example of a cross-bred used on a dude ranch; although she is only 13·2 hands high she is wiry and tough and thinks nothing of carrying twenty pounds of stock saddle and an adult rider all day. She is also adept at herding both horses and cattle—*and* she shows how to buck!

In Australia the pattern of stock horse life is much the same and the sturdy Quarter Horses have to a large degree usurped the old Waler-type animal. With their intelligence and smooth gait Quarter Horses are ideal for the long cattle droves across many thousands of miles of continent, taking anything up to two years, and they are being imported in increasing quantities.

Working for our Leisure

There are more than 2,000 riding schools in Great Britain that are licensed under the Riding School Act. This Act of Parliament has largely checked the type of place where horses and ponies, often still too immature to be ridden at all, were kept in old sheds in bad conditions and hired out cheaply to anyone. Schools that are now approved by official horse and pony organisations do an excellent job for both animals and riders. They employ qualified instructors and the grooms are often training to be instructors themselves. The horses take carefully-chosen riders; they are fed according to their individual needs and not only well-exercised but well-rested. Riding schools are rapidly coming into their own in countries such as the United States, Canada and New Zealand.

Horses and ponies also do much to help in the lives of disabled riders and there are now schools that cater solely for the disabled. Considerable physical and psychological improvement has been seen in many young disabled riders after a few weeks of riding.

Trekking is becoming a popular pursuit for those who wish to exchange the noise of the roads for the quietness of the type of countryside inaccessible to motorists. In Britain there are hundreds of trekking centres, many of which are suitable for the whole family. Treks can last for hours or for days; the trekker's normal pace is a walk and the British native ponies can easily carry an adult.

It is also possible to tour on spirited horses through Spain and Portugal, or across the puszta of Hungary, or up the Tyrolean mountains.

More than 2000 licenced riding schools in Britain provide work for around 20,000 horses; others work in forests where even the most agile tractor cannot manœuvre. In Britain a few pit ponies remain at work underground, but in the more remote parts of Europe, ponies and mules are still common transport.

Pit Ponies

Less than a dozen years ago over 10,000 ponies were working underground in British coal mines, but the number has been greatly reduced by mechanisation and now only a handful are used.

Working in a coal mine is by no means an ideal existence for ponies but they receive excellent care and have been strictly protected for years by the Coal Mines Act.

The miners take intense pride in their ponies; now they haul supplies in light trucks instead of the old coal tubs, their stalls are ventilated by intakes of fresh air and the food is protected from dust. When pensioned off they retire to 'homes of rest', or to good private homes, provided that their new owners guarantee that their pony will never have to work again.

Police Horses

Police horses are still in use in many parts of the world, even in crowded New York where some of the city's 270 mounted policemen help daily to disentangle the traffic. The main duties of the police horses are traffic control, town and country patrol and promoting good relations with the public, but perhaps their most spectacular duty is crowd control, since crowds tend to be more in awe of the horse than the policeman.

Police horses are put through a rigorous training for their job. There is very little that will upset a police horse; he is trained to ignore loud bangs, shouts and the emotional impact of crowds; he will even disregard an umbrella being opened up in his face!

Training takes about six or seven months and is undertaken by officers chosen for their patience and firmness, as well as their riding ability and experience. Since 1948, it has been a police horse of London's Metropolitan Mounted Police that has had the honour of carrying the Queen at her official Birthday Parade, the Trooping of the Colour.

In Iran, the Tehran Mounted Police ride spirited stallions, as do the mounted division of Spain's Barcelona Municipal Police, whose Andalusian horses carry out not only their normal day-to-day duties, including a unique crowd-control technique of a reverse advance with hind heels at the ready, but also give public displays of dressage and a celebrated Carousel where the stallions exhibit obedience and schooling of the highest standard. The Lesotho Police Force is the only fully mounted one in the world, using tough little countrybred ponies for their patrols over rough and mountainous terrain . . .

The day of the working horse is by no means over. They are still put to varied uses in all parts of the world and indeed, in countries such as Great Britain they are again finding their place in everyday life, when the soft puffing of a plough horse on a steep slope is an infinitely preferable sound to the roar of a tractor; and a holiday in Ireland with a skewbald mare and gypsy caravan is far more memorable than one with a noisy car skidding on the muddy roads.

Left and right: The Royal Canadian Mounted Police still use their horses over difficult terrain, although most circumstances now demand mechanised vehicles. **Above:** in London a small corps of mounted police operates in the city, now assisted by a woman's section.

What the Breed Society says: **Shire**

Original Habitat:	Leicestershire, Staffordshire, Derbyshire, although the greater number are now found in the Northern counties of England, in East Anglia and Wales.
Colour:	Black, bay or grey: usually with white feathers and markings.
Height:	16·2 to 17·2 h.h. Occasionally grow to 18 h.h.
Head and Eyes:	Head is lean in proportion to the body, neither too large nor too small. Eyes are large, prominent and docile in expression.
Neck:	Fairly long, slightly arched and well set on, to give a commanding appearance.
Body:	Back is short, strong and muscular; loins standing well.
Forehand:	Wide across the chest, but with legs well under the body and well developed in muscle.
Hindquarters:	Long and sweeping, wide and full of muscle, well let down towards the thighs.
Legs and Feet:	The sinews of the legs should be clean-cut and hard, like fine cords to touch, and clear of the cannon bones. Feet are deep, solid and not too wide, with thick walls and open coronets.
Breed Society:	The Shire Horse Society, The Showground, Alwalton, Peterborough, England.

New York, too, has its mounted police, used for crowd control and occasional traffic point-duty. **Above:** RCMP riders line up for their famous Musical Ride. **Opposite page:** the sun blazes down on Spanish mule and rider; two Austrian horses in the Alps pose for the camera; a Russian troika (three-horse vehicle) trots through the snow.

What the Breed Society says: **Percheron**

Original Habitat:	The La Perche region of France.
Colour:	Grey or black, with a minimum of white. No other colour in stallions is eligible for entry in the stud book. Skin and coat should be of fine quality.
Height:	Stallions should not be less than 16·3 h.h. and mares not less than 16·1 h.h. but, at maturity, width and depth must not be sacrificed to height.
Head:	Wide across the eyes, which should be full and docile, ears medium size and erect, deep cheek, curved on lower side, not long from eye to nose, intelligent expression.
Body:	Strong neck, not short, with full arched crest in stallions. Wide chest, deep, well-laid shoulders; back strong and short, ribs wide and deep, and deep at flank. Hindquarters of exceptional width and long from hips to tail, avoiding any suggestion of goose rump.
Limbs:	Strong arms and full second thighs, big knees and broad hocks; heavy flat bone, short cannons, pasterns of medium length, feet of reasonable size, of good quality and hard blue horn. Limbs as clean and free from hair as possible.
Action:	Straight, bold, with a long free stride, rather than a short, snappy action. Hocks well flexed and kept close. Average weight in stallions, 18–20 cwts. mares 16–18 cwts.
Breed Society:	British Percheron Horse Society, Owen Webb House, Gresham Road, Cambridge, England.

What the Breed Society says: **Clydesdale**

Original Habitat: Flanders, in Belgium. In the 19th Century some stallions were brought over to improve the native breed in Clydesdale, Scotland (now known as Lanarkshire). A Clydesdale stud book was first published in 1887.

Colour: Dark brown, black with white stripe on the face, dark-coloured fore legs and white hind shanks.

Height: 16·2 to 17·2 h.h.

Head and Eyes: An open forehead, broad between the eyes, a flat profile (neither Roman nor dished), wide muzzle, large nostrils, bright intelligent eyes and large ears. The neck should be long and springing out of an oblique shoulder, with high withers.

Body: The back should be short and ribs well sprung from the backbone, like the hoops of a barrel. Quarters should be long and well packed with muscle and sinew. Broad, clean, sharply developed hocks with big knees broad in front.

Feet: Open and round, like a mason's mallet. Hoof heads wide and springy with no suspicion of hardness that may lead to the formation of sidebones or ringbone.

Breed Society: The Clydesdale Horse Society, 19 Hillington Gardens, Glasgow S.W.2, Scotland.

Opposite page: Badminton, England — two Whitbread horses play their part in keeping the kids happy. **Above:** working horses in Spain; in an English riding school — and off duty in the Swiss snow.

What the Breed Society says: Suffolk Punch

Original Habitat:	East Anglia. Unbroken male line can be traced back to the early 18th Century, and the breed has been mentioned as far back as 1506.
Colour:	Chestnut only. There are seven shades, ranging from dark (approaching brown-black) to bright chestnut. A star, a little white on the face, or a few silver hairs are acceptable.
Height:	About 16 h.h.
Head:	Rather large, thick through the gullet. Eyes are small, not prominent and ears are also small, and point towards each other at the tips. The neck is deep in collar and tapering towards the setting of the head.
Body:	Shoulders are long and muscular, well thrown back at the withers. Deep round-ribbed from shoulder to flank, with graceful outline, in back, loin and quarters.
Legs and Feet:	Legs should be straight with fair sloping pasterns, big knees and clean long hocks on short cannon bones, free of coarse hair. Feet have plenty of size, with circular form protecting the frog.
Breed Society:	The Suffolk Horse Society, 6 Church Street, Woodbridge, Suffolk, England.

Sports-Time

The role has changed. Once the horse was used as a beast of work, a pack animal, as personal transport for travellers, a puller of cart or carriage, a farm worker. The horse was essential to daily routine, and was very much part of the everyday scene. Today he plays a different part in our lives. Since the beginning of the 20th Century, when the internal-combustion motor took over as the general source of energy on road and field, the horse has entered our leisure time in no small way. His strength, his agility, stamina, friendly temperament, are qualities which have sustained him for centuries—and now he employs them in sporting activities. Mounted sports grow in numbers as do riders and enthusiasts. And, no doubt, the horse at this point in time has a better life, healthier and more pleasant, than ever before in his history.

Some horse sports have attracted tens of thousands of *afficionados* recently. Show jumping, pony-games, horse trials, dressage; from local show to international event, crowds flock in to compete or to watch. It's not all competitive of course, and by far the greater number of riders just *ride*. Hacking, pony-trekking, mounted holidays, are all capturing the imagination of those who feel the need to vacate the town and occasionally savour the peace and tranquility of the countryside—and there is no better way to enjoy that than in the saddle of a horse or pony . . .

The sporting horse. His strength, agility, stamina, friendly temperament — are all essentials in horse trials (some call it eventing) trekking, trotting, polo…

. . . racing, driving **(opposite page, lower left)**,
hunting, tent-pegging **(below)** or just jumping
over fences with no hands!

All the Queen's Horses

The horses that draw the Queen of England's carriage on great occasions are, almost without exception, greys. These are the famous Windsor Greys—not a specific breed, but named after the grey ponies that once transported Queen Victoria round the royal parks at Windsor Castle.

It had become a tradition to keep grey horses at Windsor, the Queen's castle home 25 miles from London, but after the reign of George V they were brought to London, to take precedence over the bays which had by then replaced the former royal blacks and creams.

These horses are certainly accustomed to ceremony; it was four Windsor Greys that drew the Glass Coach used on the Queen's and Prince Philip's wedding day in 1947; eight of them, postillion ridden and controlled, manipulated the four-ton weight of the magnificent Gold State Coach when Her Majesty processed through the London streets on the day of her coronation in 1953; and the Windsor Greys have the place of honour at yearly traditional ceremonies such as the State Opening of Parliament, when the Queen drives out in the Irish State Coach. Most years some of these horses return to Windsor during Royal Ascot Week, four of them for use with an Ascot landau (a four-wheeled carriage with a folding top) when the Queen and Prince Philip lead the procession up the course before the day's horse racing.

Opposite page: the Queen's State Landau with its team of six Greys. **Above and left:** the Queen's Head coachman with Tedder, one of the Windsor Greys; the Greys in training; in the Royal Mews, and a private carriage at Windsor.

Windsor Greys are all sturdy harness types, of necessity imperturbable by nature and by training. Like all the horses kept at the Royal mews behind Buckingham Palace they are frequently driven out amongst the heavy London traffic, and are given a regular taste of the loud music and other frightening noises that go with ceremonies, from records played within the confines of the covered school.

The Greys may be Irish bred, or of any breeding that produces the right stamp, including one or two that are part-Percheron. There is now a Royal team of grey Oldenburgs, a German breed revived after World War II, and in 1971 these animals won the Concours d'Elegance at a driving competition in Hungary, organised by Prince Philip and the Crown Equerry.

From Pack-horse Work to Royal Mews

The rest of the Royal harness horses are bays. These draw the majority of the carriages in processions, convey the regalia to the opening of Parliament, and do work such as taking new Ambassadors to present their credentials to the Queen, or bring other distinguished visitors to Buckingham Palace when ceremony is required.

When the Queen and Prince Philip paid a state visit to York in 1971 they broke with tradition by using four Cleveland Bays instead of Windsor Greys—in deference to the district where these horses originated. Up to a few years ago most of the bays in the Royal mews were

Gelderlands, a Dutch breed. Now, although some of the Dutch horses remain, the majority are pure or part-bred Cleveland Bays, handsome descendants of sturdy pack horses once used by Yorkshire pedlars, bred through the years with a percentage of thoroughbred blood. The Queen owns a very successful Cleveland Bay stallion called Mulgrave Supreme, who has sired many good hunters, jumpers and harness horses.

All the horses housed in the Royal mews, those beautiful stables, harness rooms and coach houses that, like the covered school that forms part of the complex, were designed for King George IV in 1825, are State owned; but there are *other* Royal horses that belong to the Queen.

The Racing Queen

Most people in Britain know that Queen Elizabeth II enjoys racing, but her appreciation and understanding of the sport goes much deeper than just the thrills of the course. She is herself an owner, usually with about a dozen horses in training. Her celebrated stallion, Auriole, has sired many winners of famous races, and she is part owner of the well-known sire, Ribero.

The Royal mares and foals are shared between Hampton Court and another stud nearby, and the Queen often drives over from Windsor to see and discuss them with her racing manager. Through the years the Queen's interest in breeding thoroughbreds has developed into an authoritative knowledge of the intricate patterns of thoroughbred blood lines, and she is now one of the few world experts on the subject.

Queen Elizabeth herself always works out the breeding programme for each of her mares, and eventually has the fun and excitement of following and advising on the racing careers of horses that are the direct results of her own decisions. And basically it is horses, as individuals, that are the main attraction in her hobby.

The Queen; ceremonial occasion, private drive, and riding at Badminton.

Up at Balmoral Castle in Scotland the Queen knows each of the Highland and Fell ponies that are kept for shooting and stalking, as well as she knows her thoroughbred mares, and takes an equal interest in their welfare and breeding. And she likes to see for herself how the attractive pair of Haflinger mountain ponies—presented to her on a recent visit to Austria—are shaping up to the same kind of work.

Doublet-'Outsize' Winner

Several of the state carriage horses are a result of the Queen's horse-breeding enterprises at Sandringham, her country home, and a number of Prince Philip's ex-polo pony mares are kept at stud there. It was always the Queen's ambition to produce good polo ponies, but unfortunately Prince Philip seldom, if ever, seemed to get on good terms with the home-bred animals. A number also grew too big for the game, and the Prince has been heard to tease the Queen about the young stock being too well-fed. However, in Doublet, an offspring of a favourite polo pony mare, she certainly got a winner with at least one of the 'outsizes'.

This is the handsome chestnut horse that the Queen gave her daughter Princess Anne, after she had come fifth with him at the tough Horse Trials at Badminton, in April 1971, and with which Anne won at Burghley, Britain's other major Three Day Event, in the same year, winning the title of European Three Day Event Champion.

105

The Princess has two or more of her mother's home bred horses in her eventing 'string'. These young greys are as inexperienced as Doublet was at the same stage, and were both sired by Colonist II—for many years a resident stallion at Sandringham—a horse that was once one of Sir Winston Churchill's most successful steeplechasers. They show a lot of jumping ability and promise and have acquitted themselves well with the Princess in novice classes, but they are exuberant characters and the larger of the two is not always liable to remain within the limits of the dressage arena.

The Princess keeps her eventing horses with Alison Oliver (wife of the well-known show jumper Alan Oliver), who helps her train and school, but High Jinks, the well-loved pony that Anne rode with success in Pony Club competitions, is housed with the Queen's riding horses in the mews at Windsor—and is still frequently ridden round the Royal estates.

The riding horses have usually been a mixed bunch, often gifts given at State visits. *Sultan*, one of the Queen's favourites for many years, was a thoroughbred from Pakistan; *Bussaco*, a delightful stallion now on loan to a stud, came from Portugal. *Mele Kush* of the famed Akhal Teke desert breed, was presented to Prince Philip by the late Mr Khruschev. *Pride*, still an honoured inmate of the mews, hails from Jordan.

Some of the animals have come from the race-course. *Royal Worcester*, a tough old horse that is still going strong, was bred by the late King George VI as a steeplechaser—but refused to 'chase'! *Villefranche* was one of the Queen Mother's 'chasers, and *Agreement*, no longer around but a one-time favourite of Princess Margaret, was one of the Queen's more eminent race-horses, who counted the Chester Vase and Doncaster Cup amongst his numerous successes.

For many years *Betsy*, a black mare of more personality than blue-blood, was undisputed 'Number One' at Windsor, but nowadays the Queen counts another black mare amongst her favourites. Not that *Burmese* is plebian for she was bred at Fort Walsh, in Canada, one of the quality black horses produced by using thoroughbred sires with half-breed mares, to fill the ranks of the celebrated Musical Ride still performed by members of the Royal Canadian Mounted Police. The mare was presented to the Queen by the Mounties a few years ago and has proved a most versatile animal. For most of the year she performs as a mannered, willing hack for the Queen to ride round the parks and estates, but in early June Burmese goes on parade—ridden side-saddle by the Queen at the annual ceremony in London of Trooping the Colour.

As well as Burmese the Queen particularly enjoys riding *Bellboy* and *Cossack*. Both are home bred, but the aptly named Cossack, an animal of strong and engaging personality, is by *Zaman*, a lively little golden stallion from Russia that was given to Prince Charles.

Queen Elizabeth tries to find time to ride most weekends, perhaps over Easter at Windsor, during the summer holiday in Scotland and at Sandringham after Christmas. She leads a very exacting life, and horses, whether harness animals, thoroughbred brood mares, Fell and High-land ponies or those she keeps for her own riding, provide an interest and a relaxation that are as much a necessity as a pleasure.

The Irish State Coach at Buckingham Palace Mews.

Scottish Born and Bred

The Scottish native pony breeds are from the Northern part of the country, and a small group of islands way off the north coast.

The northern half of Scotland, the Highlands, still has its lonely, wild tracts of land, impossible to develop industrially, and retaining all the conditions required for ponies in their natural habitat.

In the Shetland Isles, often bleak and cold, the pony—the tiny Shetland breed—is still of use to man in his daily routine, although by far the greater number are used by children as leisure mounts.

The Highland Pony

There are two types, the larger, bred on the mainland, and the smaller Highland bred on the many isles that make up the Hebrides off the west coast of Scotland; an area which is known to many only because of the numerous gale-and-severe-weather warnings given for the area on radio. Here only the strongest are able to survive.

Semi-wild Highland ponies on the hills of Scotland.

It is claimed that the mainland pony has connections with the Celtic pony, but there is no proof of this, although archeologists have found bones which date back to the Stone Age. It is still debatable whether these ponies originated in Scotland, whether they were driven north or, as seems most likely, they originated in the Scandinavian countries and were left behind after the British Isles had become detached from the rest of Europe.

Many a visitor to the Highlands for deer stalking or grouse shooting in the autumn will be accompanied by one of these ponies, for they stand between 13·0 h.h. and 14·2 h.h.; low enough for a shot stag to be loaded onto their backs. For grouse shooting the ponies carry panniers or baskets into which the birds are put. The Highland's continued popularity for this work is due to the fact that most of the country is inaccessible even to motor vehicles, and a pony is still the best transport. It is immensely strong and will pick its way across country, and is intelligent enough not to tread on any boggy ground unable to carry its own weight. The Highland pony is also still used by some farmers or shepherds to do the rounds of their stock, and for timber-hauling by foresters.

In recent years pony trekking has become very popular. It is the ideal way to enjoy fresh air and the magnificent sights of the otherwise unseen beauty of hills, glens and lochs. Many of these pony trekking visitors will have never ridden before, and the Highland pony is the perfect animal to give them confidence and enjoyment, with its pleasant temperament, reliability and friendliness. Highland ponies also vary tremendously in size, so all riders are able to find the right mount.

Breed Description

Height:	From 13 h.h. to 14·2 h.h.
Colour:	Various, many shades of dun, i.e., yellow, cream and mouse; most ponies have zebra markings on the forelegs and a black dorsal stripe, greys are numerous and there are also blacks and browns.
Head:	Well carried, attractive and broad between bright and kindly eyes and short between eyes and muzzle with wide nostrils.
Neck:	The neck should be strong and not short, arched with a flowing mane, the throat being clean and not fleshy.
Shoulders:	These should be well set back.
Body:	The back should have a slight natural curve, with deep chest, deep ribs well-sprung and carried well back. The quarters should be powerful with strong thighs.
Legs:	The legs should be flat in bone with a slight fringe of straight silken feather ending in a prominent tuft at the fetlock joint, the forelegs should be well placed under the weight of the body; the forearm should be strong and the knee broad; pasterns oblique, must not be too short, with broad, firm, dark hooves.
Hocks:	The hocks must be broad, flat, clean and closely set.
Tail:	This should be carried gaily.

Tall and the short — a tiny Shetland pony is examined by a large working horse. **Below:** Shetland pony and foal.

The Shetland Pony

'See the smallest pony in the world', the English fairground (carny) barkers used to shout. And on paying their few pence admission charge the customers would find a fairly small Shetland Pony. The Shetland is the most popular breed in Britain and is little larger than a Great Dane. Some people even allow them into the kitchen to lie in front of the fire just like a pet dog. However, although very small and docile the Shetland is immensely strong for its size, and extremely hardy—a sort of miniature draught horse . . .

It is said that when Sir Francis Drake left his game of bowls at Plymouth Hoe, and set out to smash the Spanish Armada in 1588, many of the Spanish ships were carrying stallions. As the Spanish ships foundered, these swam ashore—and helped to improve the local stock in the Shetland Isles. That's the romantic legend; it is far more likely that the pony is descended from Norwegian stock.

Long ago in England, children were used as 'beasts of draught', and were made to work down the coal mines, hauling the coal from the face. However, by an Act in Parliament in 1840, this was stopped, and a different 'beast of draught' had to be found. Shetland ponies provided the solution because of their small size and great durability.

The breed has become crossed with other types of pony in only a few instances, and it is simple enough to pick out the cross-breeds from the true Shetland, as ever since the Breed Society was formed in 1890 the births of pure bred ponies have been carefully recorded.

In the Shetland Isles the pony was often the only method of transport (and still is, occasionally) and it was common for a pony to carry a man forty miles a day. The 'Sheltie', as the pony is affectionately known, carried seaweed to the farms, to be used as a fertiliser, and it was also tough enough to pull plough or harrow, with a hardiness built up over countless generations of cold winters, when it lived only on seaweed, and wandered over the pitiless moors.

Prize-winning Shetland, foal, and young owner at a national show. **Right:** Shetlands are often used in the circus ring for their temperament and their appeal.

Breed Description

Height: Registered stock must not exceed 40 inches at three years old or 42 inches at four years old and over.

Colour: Black or any other known colour in horses.

Coat: The coat changes according to the seasons of the year; double coat in winter and smooth in summer.

Head: The head should be small and well-shaped, broad between the eyes, and with small well-placed ears; the eyes should be dark and intelligent.

Neck: The neck should have a good crest, especially in stallions, be strong and muscular, and rise off a well-laid oblique shoulder.

Body: The body should have deep-sprung ribs, short back, with broad chest and strong quarters. The tail should be profuse and set fairly high. The loins should be strong and muscular.

Legs: The forelegs should be well-placed under the shoulders, with well-muscled forearm and strong knees, followed by broad, flat bone, and springy pasterns. The hindlegs should have strong and muscular thighs, with broad, clean hock and broad, flat bone with springy pasterns.

Feet: The feet should be open, round and tough.

Action: The action should be free and true, with each joint freely used.

Portrait of a Highland pony. **Below:** a pit-pony and his groom. **Right:** trekking in the Scottish Highlands.

World Apart—the Traditional Circus

The dictionary says: *Circus: a place of amusement where horsemanship and acrobatic feats are exhibited.* Carny, circus, big top, call it what you like, it's the oldest and most breath-taking animal entertainment the world has devised, for young people and the young-in-heart, since the days when the ancient Romans watched their favourites slam two-horse chariots round the Circus Maximus.

The horse is still symbolic of the sawdust ring, that magic circle bathed in coloured spotlight. And although there are fewer horse-acts today—mainly because there are fewer circuses in this modern bustling world of mechanical entertainments—the horse still reigns supreme as a demonstration of animal talent and obedience.

Modern equestrian acts date as far back as Philip Astey, who first performed, in 1768, in some fields in what is now the district of Lambeth, London, where he *submitted equestrian feats for the public approval.* He performed in a circular roped ring so that all the audience could see him properly; thus was the magic circle of the show-ring born.

Then there was Phineas Taylor Barnum, perhaps the most famous showman of them all. He gave to America the 'Greatest Show on Earth' and his name was, as one American President said, 'The best-known name in the world'.

'Buffalo Bill' Colonel William Cody, hunter, scout, brought to the world his legendary 'Wild West shows', packed with horses and skilled riders and thrills for young audiences from Birmingham, Alabama to Birmingham, England.

Finally there was Billy Smart, whose travelling circus still entertains millions all over Europe. His showmanship, his animals, and particularly his horses—whose act with his grand-daughter Jasmin has transported countless young watchers into another world, the fantastic world of the circus—make one of the last great traditional entertainments in modern life.

Not exactly *Haute Ecole* perhaps, but the horsemaster comes from the Spanish Riding School in Vienna, and this is probably the best-trained troupe in Europe. **Below:** liberty horses at Billy Smart's Circus.

Opposite page: early morning rehearsal. Even the best of liberty horses must go through this every morning of the year . . . if the evening performance is to finish like this **(top)**.

The magic of the sawdust ring captures the
imagination of all ages . . .

More rehearsals **(opposite page),** and **(above)** a Shetland act which ends with the smaller horse standing on the larger. The girl is Jasmin Smart, grand-daughter of the founder of the most famous circus in Europe.

Golden Horse of the West

The fabled Golden Horse has appeared in records since the beginning of civilisation—in Asia, China and Europe. In mythology, in history, in the annals of many countries and courts, the horse that is considered by many to be the most beautiful animal in the world has been known, fêted, coveted and prized.

It is difficult to separate fiction from history, so many are the stories of this golden horse.

Greek mythology says that the horse was a gift from Poseidon, the Sea God, and the legend of the sun-and-sea horse probably begins there, way back in the mists of Ancient Greece.

The light-maned horses were probably brought to Greece by an oriental race, the Hitites, and Homer tells of the colourful Greek chariot-horses, calling them Xanthos, a word meaning something between gold and chestnut, but which is known today rather more prosaically as dun. In fact the great Achilles had two horses which he called Xanthos and Balios—*yellow as gold and swifter than storm winds* was their description.

Later in history the famous Bayeux tapestries from 11th Century France depict golden—Palomino—horses cavorting with some strange-looking blue ones. In the days of Columbus and the Spanish Court it is known that Queen Isabella had a fondness for golden horses, and at that time they were called Golden Isabellas. Thus Palominos have been found in every blood-line and combination of blood-lines all over the world.

The name Palomino is said by some to derive from the Palomino grape, and it is probable that this juicy golden grape was grown by Juan Palomino to whom conquistador Cortez gave an Isabella (called, more precisely, a Y'sabella) described as having a coat as *pure as gold of a newly minted gold coin, with a mane and tail as white as snow.*

The Palomino, this beautiful horse of the Americas, is officially described by the Palomino Horse Breeders of America, its Breed Society, as . . . *a body colour near that of an untarnished U.S. gold coin and the mane and tail are white. Skin is dark, except under white markings. Eyes are dark or hazel. White markings are permitted on the legs to the knees or hocks and on the face. The horse cannot show draft horse or pony characteristics and is over 900 pounds and 14 hands when fully grown.*

The PHBA also requires proof of breeding. The dam or sire must be registered in PHBA to be a Thoroughbred, Quarter Horse, American Saddle Horse, Arabian, Morgan, Tennessee Walker, American Remount, or Trotting Horse, all of which must have been registered with their appropriate Societies.

The PBHA select two types of Palomino for special mention: the Palomino Quarter Horse, and the American Saddlebred Palomino. Of the Quarter Horse the PBHA says . . . *outstanding for his versatility as an athlete and incomparable for his golden color. A horse registered with PHBA for his Palomino color, yet with all the characteristics of the Quarter Horse registered with the American Quarter Horse Association. The Quarter Horse was the first breed of horse developed in the Americas . . . he is not only a running horse, he is a show horse, ranch or cowhorse, cutting horse and a pleasure horse. He is versatile, gentle, intelligent, sure-footed and is loved for his easy-going disposition.*

The Palomino has appeared in myth, legend and history from earliest times. Today the PHBA states that a Palomino should be as near 15.2 hands, and 1100 lb as possible.

The PHBA call the American Saddlebred Palomino:

The aristocrat of the horse world, renowned for his beauty of color and beyond comparison for his temperament, courage and vitality. He is graceful, enduring, powerful and intelligent: But the American Saddlebred Palomino not only is all these, he also has stood the test from field, ranch and trail to battlefield and show ring.

As defined by PHBA, he stands approximately 16 hands and has thin skin with a gleaming, golden finish. Bright eyes are set well apart on a clean-cut head, ears are delicate, alert and expressive. Free of coarseness, his neck is long, fine, flexible, and arched on a sloping shoulder. The withers are fairly prominent, free of beefiness and extending well back.

His back is short and his body is deep and well-rounded with levelled hips, smoothly rounded croup and high-set tail. His legs are of fine structure with prominent tendons and smooth, well-made joints. They move as freely as a pendulum and with the grace of a dancer. Forearms and gaskins are well-developed, hocks are placed well under him to give balance and his pasterns are of a good length, set at nearly the same angle as the shoulder to give the body carriage and springiness.

The performance events of the Palomino Saddlebred include the relaxed English pleasure, the three-gaited, the fine harness, equitation, the parade and the incomparable beauty and driving speed of the five-gaited rack.

Trotting races **(opposite page)** show the
Palomino off to advantage. **Top:** a Palomino
Welsh Mountain Pony. **Above:** a Supreme in-hand
Champion, Palomino mare Kingsettle Pagoda.

None but the Brave

—*The Toughest Sport of Them All?*

However artful a dodger was that handsome, vulgar 19th Century hunting swell, Mr S. Sponge, he was certainly wise to the truth when it came to a disagreement with his horse in public. As author R. S. Surtees puts it: *If the man feels the horse has the best of it, it is wise for the man to appear to accommodate his views to those of the horse, rather than risk a defeat. It is best to let the horse go his way, and pretend it is yours.* Then, with sharp insight, Surtees advises his hero: *There is no secret so close as that between a rider and his horse.* But, unlike R. S. Surtees' other immortal foxhunter, Mr Jorrocks, *who wasn't afraid of the pace so long as there was no leaping,* Mr Sponge could, at least, find the courage to sit tight over his fences when hounds were running.

Horse and man have been finding and keeping each other's secrets for many thousands of years, but the challenge of discovery has never failed to involve each new generation of horsemen. Perhaps this constant struggle for mastery is one reason why man must forever be proving that, with his guidance, the horse can gallop over bigger and still more hair-raising obstacles across the countryside.

Whatever the explanation, there is no doubt in the minds of the growing army of three day event riders today that the more 'hairy' the fence, the more satisfying it is, for the experienced anyway, to tackle—and, of course, to describe to friends afterwards! For the uninitiated, it is

None but the Brave
These two shots are of European Three-Day Event Champion Her Royal Highness Princess Anne.
Left, on Collingwood, and **right,** Columbus.

Badminton cross-country course; here a horse takes two 'bites' at a rustic obstacle.

sometimes hard to realise that although sheer size is very intimidating, dimensions are only a problem when the natural hazards of the terrain make them so. It is the placing of the obstacle in relation to the steep slope, the awkward distanced ditch and the hidden drop, that causes the real upsets.

Cross-Country at Badminton

Since 1949, when the Duke of Beaufort turned his beautiful home and parkland in Gloucestershire over to an annual equestrian championship the Badminton Three Day Event in April has become the Mecca of international horsemen from all over the world. The course may vary, with new fences designed or old ones left out; perhaps a change in the jumping order or even a complete reversal of direction from a left-handed circuit to a right-handed one. But the landmarks, in whatever sequence they occur, are always there; the fir trees of Huntsman's Close, the yawning chasm of the Quarry, the dreadul gaping trench at the Vicarage Ditch, the Luckington Lane in-and-out rails, the treacherous Coffin, the deep-bottomed Lake . . .

By the time the action moves to the Box for the start of the Cross-Country on the second day, the previous day's Dressage test is thankfully in the past. The Speed and Endurance section, after $3\frac{1}{4}$ miles of Roads and Tracks, $2\frac{1}{4}$ miles of Steeplechase and a second $5\frac{1}{2}$ miles of roads and tracks, is three-quarters over. With the seconds ticking away before the start of the final and most difficult test there are still a couple of decisions to make. Having walked the

Top: the Normandy Bank at Badminton . . .
and a fence-and-drop at Burghley, Britain's other
international three-day event venue.

course three times to familiarise with every inch of the track, Fence 12 is still a headache. After going round the course in bed the night before, trying in vain to get some sleep, you realise the worrying fences are the ones the horse may decide to tackle in his own mysterious fashion—the ones where he may decline to listen to his jockey's plans and act on his own initiative.

Two minutes to go; it is distinctly unnerving to walk round in small, anti-social bad-tempered circles in an effort to keep busy.

That Fence 12; the way to jump it is to get into the water, but the horse might bound right across instead . . . the thoughts still circulate round a harassed mind.

One minute to go, and any decisions not made now will result in disaster. Rightly or wrongly, one of the two alternatives must become a hard plan.

The flag is up, it is suddenly important to have a clear, level head. The starter's arm drops quickly and it's too late to panic now.

It's not far to the first fence, 250 yards. Just about enough space to settle into a steady stride as the Lake drops away to the left, before swinging half right-handed up to the *Tree Trunk and Rails*. Nothing to that, but it's time to slow up for the very nasty second fence, the *Field Gate*. Coming down off the road a little too fast, the bottom of the gate arrives much too soon, as the horse is all on his forehand. This is not the way to do it, he should be back on his hocks but it's no good. There's a crash as he hits it behind, but luckily not hard enough to bring him down.

The lake at Badminton. Although each year brings a new obstacle or two, there are many traditional ones such as this. Badminton cross-country course is considered by many to be the toughest in the world.

Turning left now, and up to the trees for the first part of the *Huntsman's Close* trio. This needs riding slowly, but fast enough to get the spread in—not so easy to judge going from the open into the dark wood. Turning right-handed through the trees, there are these small rails out over a big drop, with a great big hollow ditch on the other side. The trees make a fast approach difficult, but then there's the rising ground to get out over, the other side. The horse meets it right, but lacks impulsion as he lands, hits the rising ground, and goes up on his nose out through the Christmas trees. There are only about two strides before the next lot of rails, and both the reins are on the ground along with the horse's nose. A quick recovery, and then the Christmas trees are left behind as the *Elephant Trap*, No. 6, is suddenly dead ahead.

This year it's bigger than it has ever been, but it's not really so difficult except that there's only a 50 yards run at it from the sharp right turn out of Huntsman's Close. It's just a question of stepping on the accelerator and galloping on for the rail, to clear the big ditch that stretches out underneath it. People are awed by it because it's big, but it's more of a jockey-stopper than a problem for horses, as the rails actually slope away. All the horse needs is confidence.

Then 50 yards on again is the *Cat's Cradle*, always a big problem. The posts-and-rails form two triangles, whose points meet in the middle, and the choice is whether to jump two corners or go straight down the middle. The latter course means slowing down and knocking the horse out of his stride, but the former, over the two right-hand corners proves safe, comfortable and accurate, and the horse saves his energy by taking the narrow angles of the corners in his stride. In a hazard like this, there's always a danger of running out at a corner, but the narrow angle removes the necessity to jump it so near the flag . . .

An upsloping ramp, then a deep drop down onto sloping grass — that's the Ski-jump at Badminton.

Up to her neck in water (well, the horse's neck) at a South African event; two more Badminton jumps.

Now the horse is running easily with plenty in hand as he covers the 500 yard gallop up to the *Quarry*, for there is a long way to go yet. He needs to have his wits about him here, speeding would be disastrous with that dreadful drop down over the stone wall. Useless now to remember another year when the bottom of the Quarry was filled in; there's too much to think of, sitting right back in the saddle over the drop to stop another nose-dive.

So far, the course has gone in a big loop, but now it winds down the hill back into the Park again to meet the headache of the day—Jump No. 12, a ditch followed by a rail. It sounds quite innocuous and ordinary. It's not. There's a big ditch running along the bottom of the Park, dammed up and full of water, and just the other side comes a post-and-rails. Even a hurried reconnoitre after the start, to watch how the first twelve horses approached it, had proved to be a failure as none of them got over.

A last-minute plan to go into the wet ditch, trot up the bank on the far side and pop over the rail, disintegrates when the horse decides to change his tactics midstream. Instead of trotting out, he bounds right in under the fence, too short between ditch and rail to put in a stride on the straight, and too long to jump right out over the ditch and right out again over the rail. So it's a bold question asked now, and a bold answer needed to get out at all. It is just as well there are no points deducted for awkward jumping, because the exit there was one best forgotten . . .

The dramatic *Ski Jump* and the *Normandy Bank* are behind now, and just over half-way round the course goes on up the hill, towards the Lake, to another big fence, the *Giant's Table*, by the side of the water. The horse just gallops on, hopefully, and starts to swing left-handed, jumping out of the *Deer Park* over Fence No. 17, the sunken *Park Wall*. This has become very nasty because there is a sort of platform built, to go down on to and jump the wall from, and it is very boggy. The horse goes down on his forehand, gets stuck in the bog and has an awful job to get out and over the wall. With that effort, it suddenly becomes apparent, too, that his stride is flagging a little and it's time to take a breather and put more chaotic thoughts in order.

Vicarage Ditch is huge. The crowd, having already tasted blood in earlier disasters, is muttering, but the noise dies abruptly as the steward blows his whistle and the horse enters the penalty zone. Don't hook here, ride on hard to keep the momentum going, because it's a frightening fence, but again it's a jockey-stopper. The chasm of the open ditch gapes awfully as the horse meets it, standing not too far back, and climbs on through the top of the big black hedge, about 10 ft. square. Christmas night! How on earth can he reach the top to jump over—but he takes it and it's not so much after all.

Turning right-handed now, on to the *Luckington Lane V-Rails*. Drop down into it, sharp left and sharp right, out again. No problem, provided the horse literally does just drop down, and trots up the Lane. It's about one stride, and out again, and it's not too difficult to go slowly now, because the horse is beginning to get a bit tired . . .

Gallopers and Thinkers

In eventing, there are two basic types of fences: the galloping ones, and those where the rider tells his horse: 'Pay attention, think what you're doing, this is a tricky one.' The next one's a galloper; there's a 500 yard stretch to two lovely hedges across the Centre Walk and away on to the right-handed loop round *Tom Smith's Walls*. The alternative is to jump across the corner, or jump one wall, then a stride and the other wall. Both ways are difficult, and the corner is big, but so is the right angle, and so also is a loop almost out of the penalty zone. Thank goodness that's over.

Right-handed again, now, over the *Shark's Teeth*, and the horse needs aiming at a point on the ground to give him something to take off from. It's a fair spread, but his momentum carries him on over the zig-zag rails.

The *Parallel Rails* are next, and they're deceptive because they're maximum height, maximum spread, and dead parallel. But the horse seems to make nothing of it as he sets off towards the worst fence of the course, the *Coffin*. This year, the rails are just too high and just too close in to the ditch, so that as the horse comes up to the fence it is impossible to see where he will land.

The first day of a three-day event is taken up with dressage, then day two sees the speed-and-endurance tests, and the last day is devoted to show jumping — just to prove the horses are still fit after their ordeals.

133

In fact, he lands on the slope down towards the ditch, and without pausing for breath jumps across the ditch and straight out the other side. There wasn't room to do anything else, without slowing down to a trot, popping in, scrambling down and up the other side and out. But that would have been an awful mess, whereas it was a very conscious effort to go straight in, across, and out.

The end is nearly in sight now, only three more to jump, and the difficult thing is to keep going across the boggy part of the Park to the *Whitbread Garden*, a table with a bar on the top. Hold the horse together and jump out over it, and away down to the *Lake* where so many promising rounds have ended.

It's vital to avoid the soft mud under the water and jump into the middle, but slowly, so the horse has a chance to see what he's asked to do. He *must* keep going forward and let his impulsion propel him through the water at a trot so that he always has two legs on the ground, and can take off at any time. To let him canter would be fatal, as then he'd only have his feet on the ground once in every stride, and couldn't take off so readily.

The last fence, unbelievably, looms up—rails out over the water. Trotting slowly across the Lake, the horse makes his final effort up on to the jetty, and lands thankfully out over the rails on dry ground. The crowd, denser than ever, claps excitedly and makes way for the final lap up to the Finishing Post. If that dizzy feeling in the head weren't quite so over-powering, it would be exhilarating. Instead, it's just a big relief to have stayed this Cross-Country course in one of the toughest events in the world.

Ponies of Wild Wales

Due to the geographical contours of Wales the main industrial development has taken place round the coast, leaving the hilly and mountainous country in the centre free. There, Welsh ponies have been able to continue their natural existence. It is still possible to see them being used on the farms in the hills, as they are able to reach places unapproachable by mechanised transport and plant.

Today the Welsh Pony and Cob Society divides the ponies of Wales into three distinct types (plus the Welsh Cob) each having been bred for a definite purpose. Firstly, the *Welsh Mountain Pony* (referred to as *Section A* by the Society), the smallest at 12 hands. This is acknowledged as the world's most beautiful pony and has existed in the wild area since time immemorial.

Then there's the *Welsh Pony*, size up to 13·2 h.h. This should be an enlarged edition of the Mountain pony, with, says the breed Society, the emphasis on those points which distinguish a modern riding animal. Some are, in fact, Welsh Mountain ponies that have grown over-height, others have a dash of larger blood in their make-up. As the Mountain Pony is an ideal first mount for a child, so the Welsh is the perfect next step when the first pony is outgrown.

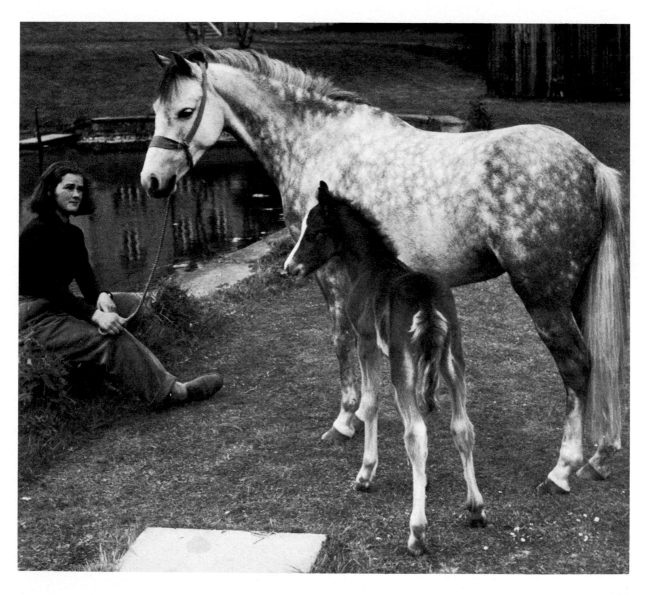

The *Welsh Pony—Cob Type* (Section C in the book is up to 13·2 h.h. and is a stronger counterpart of the Welsh pony, usually with some cob blood in his veins. Ideal for trekking and hunting, this one is surefooted and strong and always in demand.

Although covered by the same breed Society the *Welsh Cob*, at a minimum height of 13·2 h.h. exceeds, as often as not, the official pony maximum of 14·2 h.h. His foundation is the Welsh Mountain Pony and his history goes back to centuries before records were kept. He has had a great influence on trotting animals all over the world, and has been described as 'the best ride and drive animal in the world'.

General Description

Height: (a) Welsh Mountain—not exceeding 12 h.h.
           (b) Welsh Pony—not exceeding 13·2 h.h.

Colour: All colours are permitted except for piebald and skewbald, which are rigidly barred.

Head: Small and clean cut, with a fine muzzle, large bold eyes and small prick ears. Blue eyes are not uncommon and are permitted; they are usually found in very old strains.

Neck: Must be well carried and set into strong, well set shoulders.

Back: Short with strong loins, and the tail set well and gaily carried.

Limbs: Clean, flat bone with substance, strong forearms and short cannon bones. Good strong well let down hocks.

Feet: Round and hard, a reasonable amount of 'silky' feather is permitted, as in all hill stock subjected to hard climatic conditions.

Welsh Cob

Height: From 14 h.h. to 15·2 h.h. average, though no upper limit.

Head: Characteristic of all Welsh breeds, with the slightly dished Arab-type face.

Character: Welsh Cobs should have strength and quality and great freedom of action in all paces. In the past long-distance trotters, today they are mostly riding animals. They make fine jumpers, with courage and agility, and good hunters. A hardy constitution allows the Welsh Cob to live out and, compared with many, it is economical to keep.

A Welsh Mountain pony, Coed Coch Pryderi.

Before You Buy . . .

If your knowledge is limited, it is usually an easy matter to find a good vet to advise you on soundness and conformation. It is not always so easy to get similar advice on suitability. So many horses are spoiled, and riders discouraged, through the combination of horse and rider being entirely unsuited temperamentally to each other. One often sees a horse or pony in the hunting field, show-ring, or event-field which is in no way a beauty, and might be all wrong, conformation-wise, and yet he knows his job perfectly and is the ideal schoolmaster for the beginner. On the other hand it is just as common to see a really showy type of horse with perfect conformation, which is totally unsuitable for a beginner, being either bad-mannered or hot-headed.

First, Look For . . .

Now in order of importance let us look at our likely choice for a novice rider. As we have agreed, whatever form our riding is going to take, one of the most important factors in choosing our horse is his temperament, and how it is going to fit in with our own. A hot horse and a hot rider seldom get on together, and so many good-looking flashy horses tend to hot up when you really start to work and school them. This in no way means that they are not good horses, only that they will need a cool head and careful schooling to get the best out of them. They are therefore obviously more suited to the experienced, knowledgeable rider than to the novice.

Next, balance. A naturally well-balanced horse is usually a good ride and an easy ride. If he moves well it will enable us to ride him well, and this means we will enjoy working with him. It is as well to remember here that in training our horse we are simply teaching him to carry out his natural movements at the command of the rider on his back. Even the high-school movements 'on' and 'above' the ground are only reproducing the natural paces of a horse playing in a field, so it stands to reason that a well-balanced free mover will be easier to school on.

Let's assume you are going to see a horse with a view to purchase. Here are a few points to bear in mind. Have the animal brought out of the stable and stand him up square. Watch how he comes out. Does he come out with a purpose, and stand alert, showing an interest in his surroundings? Does he charge out, and then fidget around? Or does he have to be dragged out; and then stand with his head on the ground?

Inspection: *Head First*

Now have a look over him. The best way to do this is as you would read a book, begin at the beginning and work your way to the end. Starting with his head then; it need not be a 'pretty' head, but does it show kindness and intelligence? The eyes will tell you a great deal, and should be big and bold, with plenty of width between them. Is the head well set on to the neck or is it 'upside down'? Is it in keeping with the rest of his body, not too large or too small? Has he enough room in the throat or gullet? If he is cramped or restricted here it could affect his breathing. Have a look in his mouth to make sure he is not parrot-mouthed (when the upper and lower jaws do not meet as they should).

Neck:

The neck should leave the shoulder in a slight arch to the poll. It should not be too thick and heavy and should show good 'length of rein'. A neck that is too thick and heavy on the underside generally means that the horse's action will be cramped, and he will carry his head too high. This in turn will hollow his back and make it hard for the rider to 'sit into' him.

Left: a short, thick neck. **Centre:** straight, loaded shoulder with long neck. **Right:** a common head, ewe-neck combined with straight shoulder.

Shoulders:

The shoulders should be fine, not thick and 'stuffy', with a good slope on them. This can be seen best from the side, but make sure you also have a look from the front to see he has enough room in the chest and that his front legs are not too close together. Remember that the front and back to the girth play a very important part in control and balance. A heavy neck and thick shoulder could mean the horse will go on his forehand, which means he will be un-balanced and heavy in the hands.

Girth and Back:

Behind the shoulder the girth should be deep with plenty of 'heart-room'. The ribs should be well sprung, but not barrel-ribbed (over-round). He should have a good strong back, but here we have to consider the job we have in mind for him. A short back usually means an active animal and a good jumper, but a long back could mean a better mover and a more comfortable ride.

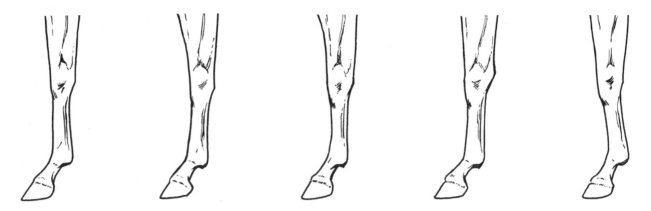

Left to right: light on bone; 'tied in' below the knees. Small, calf knees 'back at the knee'. A good foreleg. Another, with well-developed trapezium bone. 'Over at the knee' which is no real fault, but with a slightly 'appley' fetlock.

Loins, Quarters and Hocks:

Strength is of the utmost importance as it is from here that we get impulsion and power. For a jumper it is not a fault if the quarters slope a little. The hocks should also show strength and not be coarse or bony. The tail should be well set on so that the horse can carry it when moving.

Legs and feet:

Without good, sound legs and feet your horse will be no use to anyone, so here you must be particularly careful. Unless one is really knowledgeable it is essential to get expert veterinary advice on the legs and feet, as it is these which have to bear the greatest strain and wear. The horse should stand straight and square on his legs. He should have bone enough to carry his own weight and that of his rider, and the bone should be strong and flat; beware of rounded joints. See that the tendons and ligaments are clear and distinct, and the legs cool, with no sign of filling around the joints.

Feet must be even in size, and neither too big and flat, nor too small and boxy. The horn should look healthy, not brittle and shell-like. The frog is important as this is the cushion of the foot; it must be pliable, not hard and contracted.

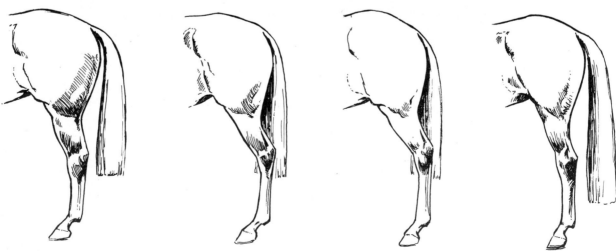

Left to right: a good hind leg. Sickle hocks and 'tied in' above the hock. Sickle hocks 'standing away' and 'up in the air'. Over-straight hocks.

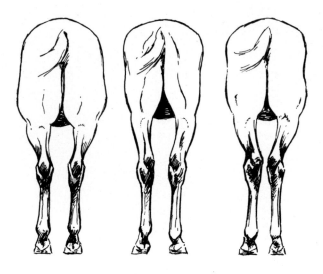

Left to right: a 'Good 'un' to follow. Split up behind, hocks in the air. A pair of cow-hocks.

Movement

First have him walk straight, away from you and back again, and then see him trot the same way. Make sure he does not 'dish' or 'plait', and also that he does not move too close in front or behind as this means he will brush and hit himself, causing splints and other blemishes.

The Ridden Horse

First try to assess the demonstrator-rider's ability. If you decide he is more competent than you, take this into consideration, as he is probably getting the best out of the horse. Watch how he rides him. Does he have to work hard to show him off to advantage? Is he sitting quiet and still to prevent the horse from hotting up? Is the horse taking a strong hold or is he having to be kicked along? Try to decide how well schooled he is, and how much you think you can improve him. Is he happy and relaxed in his work, or does he look sour with his ears back and his tail swishing? It is a good idea to ask the rider to gallop him and then see whether he will pull up and walk off quietly on a loose rein.

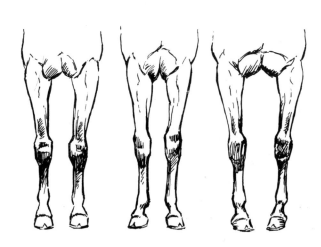

Left to right: good front; short strong cannons. Both legs 'coming out of one hole', turned out feet and light on bone. 'Boosomy' and pigeon-toed.

Now Ride Him Yourself

Having seen him ridden you should have a fair idea of how he goes. Don't be too ambitious and ask too much of him too quickly; now is the time to find out if you are going to suit each other, and if you are going to be able to manage him. Ask yourself if he is the right type and size for you, and if he will do the job you have in mind for him.

When a decision has been taken and you have agreed on price, have him vetted by a reputable horse vet. Tell him about any lumps or bumps you may have noticed, or if you have any suspicions about the horse's wind. Tell him what sort of work you are going to do with the animal. If he has already done a fair 'mileage' the vet may advise X-raying the feet and front joints, as this is the only sure way of telling how sound he is. He will also make a careful check of wind, eyes, heart and limbs.

When you have received a favourable report from your vet, and *before taking delivery of your new purchase*, you would do well to find out as much as possible from the previous owner about the amount and type of exercise and feed the horse has been having. A drastic change in a horse's diet and routine can often cause trouble. Get to know your horse first, and then make any changes you consider necessary.

Finally, if you intend to specialise in any particular branch of equestrianism, it is a tremendous help to have the assistance 'on the ground' of someone experienced. In most cases a knowledgeable onlooker will be able to put right minor faults before they become bad habits.

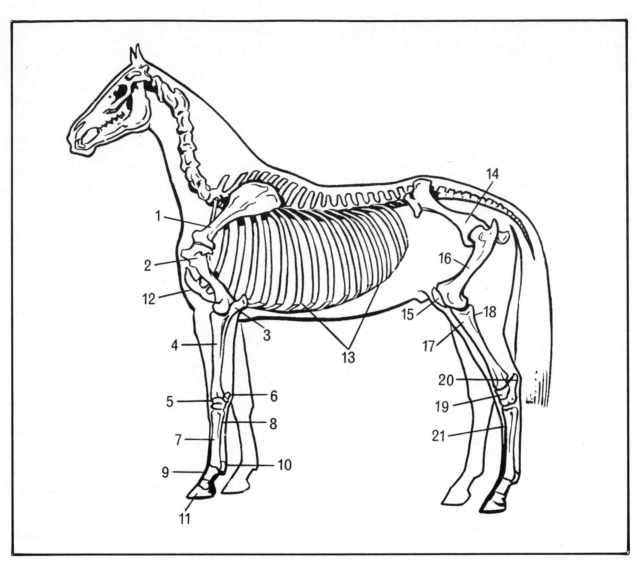

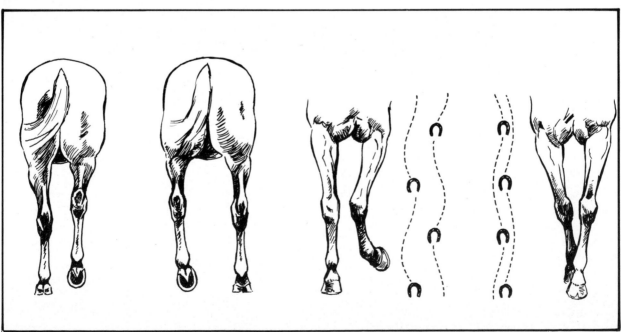

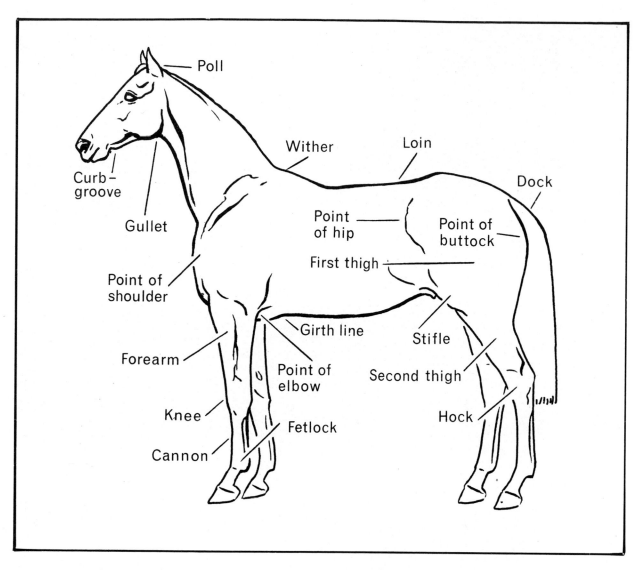

Labels on the diagram:

Poll

Curb-groove

Gullet

Point of shoulder

Forearm

Knee

Cannon

Fetlock

Wither

Point of hip

Girth line

Point of elbow

Loin

Point of buttock

First thigh

Stifle

Second thigh

Hock

Dock

Above and above left: the skeleton and points of the horse. Key to the skeleton:

1 Scapula
2 Humerus
3 Ulna
4 Radius
5 Carpus
6 Trapezium
7 Metacarpal
8 Splint bones
9 Pastern
10 Sesamoid bones
11 Coffin bones
12 Sternum
13 True and false ribs
14 Pelvis
15 Patella
16 Femur
17 Tibia
18 Fibula
19 Tarsus
20 Os Calcis
21 Metatarsal

Diagrams for this chapter are reproduced with kind permission from *Handbook of Showing* by Glenda Spooner, Museum Press, London.

Far left: a straight mover, and a horse going wide behind. **Left**: dishing action, and plaiting.

"The grace, the pace,
the elegance,
the skill and discipline are
all here embodied in the art of High School,
from the salute to the closing of the doors."

Ludwig Fischer, 1832.